Thank you, Joel. "We a team."

He Was A Boy Who Smiled. Book One: Phoenix Rising.

Copyright 2018 by Michael Stoneburner

Editor: Rita Hart

Cover Art: Hayden Fryer

Cover Design: Kaeden James

This is a book of memories expressed by the author and presented with recollections happening over time. Some names and characteristics have changed, some events have been condensed and some dialogue has been recreated.

ISBN-13: 978-0-646-80048-6

He Was A Boy Who Smiled

Book One: Phoenix Rising

Michael Stoneburner

Table of Contents

Prologue

Dear Michael,

There were a few questions you wanted to hear growing up from the adults and you never were asked. I know I'm 30 years too late but I want to ask them.

"Are you okay? Do you need help?"

We both know the answers to those questions.

"No. I am not okay. Yes, I really do need help."

How good would it have been if the adults in our lives had asked those questions and changed everything that happened? How great would it have been to see an adult take action and actually save us?

Or hear an adult say, "I believe you."

But they didn't. That's not the truth. The truth is you did it on your own. As I wrote our story, Michael, I'd realise just how much of a hero we were to ourselves. You are a survivor. We survived. You stood on your own two feet no matter how small you were, how young you were or how right or wrong you were.

You did that for me so that I could grow up and tell our story so no one else would be alone. They'd have us instead of having nothing or they'd see that they had the power to save themselves.

You just kept going and I recognize that now and soon others will too. You wanted to be inspired. You wanted someone to tell you it was okay to be you. You wanted your hopes and your dreams.

You grew up with an alcoholic father who had you when he was 19 years old. Your mother was 20. They met and within two weeks of knowing each other, they married. During your father's drunken nights, even before you started school, you were told how much of a burden you were, how much of a mistake you were and that you were the curse of the first born. You had a mother who let this all happen as she survived his wrath as well.

7

At school, you were reminded about how wrong you were and how different, from being left-handed, to disrespecting adults by asking why and enjoying the other boys' smiles. I know you're not okay and you won't be for a long time.

I wish you could know just how strong you are and how brave you are. I wish you could see how you were your own hero and that you did have support and helpers, in a cat, in a grandmother and in the imagination that took you out of the nightmare of your life and put you into beautiful dreams. You dreamt of becoming like someone like me.

I want to thank you. Thank you for saving us. Thank you for stepping in and righting as many wrongs as you could and those that you shouldn't have had to do. Thank you for being compassionate and loving, for questioning your actions and knowing at such a young age that growing up to be a Shadow Monster, a bully, an enabler or just giving up wasn't an option for you. I'm breathing today because of you.

You were silenced then, but I am your voice now. I tell your story so that others will get that voice, too. To think, you'd rise out of the ashes and be that phoenix you always wanted to be.

Love, Michael

P.S. I'm still using my left hand. I still hold my pencil differently. I still ask why when I don't understand where people are coming from. I still put my left hand on my heart if saying the pledge of allegiance and I still enjoy another man's smile.

When I Drowned

"Nothing but the best for you," my father said as he helped me organise a change of clothes, a little box full of crayons, and some paper. He had bought all these things for my first day of school even though my mom told him not to worry too much. "Your uncle had wanted to give me their old crib, but I said no. I had to buy you a brand new one. You're my son. My firstborn."

My baby brother used that crib now. I'd had my own bed for a while. I was going to be five in the summer. I didn't fit in the crib any longer. I had tried. A big bed was more comfortable, anyway. I told Christopher, as he cooed up at me, that when he was bigger he could share my bed. There would be plenty of room, and we could play toys any time we liked.

I climbed up onto my rocking horse and swayed backwards and forwards on it while my dad packed my schoolbag at the foot of my bed. Whiskey darted one of her white tipped paws out to attack my dad from beneath the bed. He jumped a bit each time and laughed.

"Your cat is crazy," he said.

I nodded my head with the rocking horse and said, "She picked me."

"She did," he said and dared to stick a finger where the bed sheets touched the floor. A small paw came out and batted at him. "At the Crowell Farm back in Tucson, Arizona, she was in a barrel with a litter of other kittens and you went over to the barrel wanting to see. You could hear them mewing."

I stopped rocking and listened. I loved hearing this story even though it only happened about a month ago. Whiskers peaked her head out too. She must have loved to hear the story, too. Most of her fur was black with white speckled throughout her fur except for a large patch of butterscotch fur that looked like someone has splashed paint on her side.

"I lifted you up, so you could see, and suddenly one little kitten started jumping up onto the edge of a deep wooden barrel. She had the longest whiskers I had ever seen. Twice as long as her head. I put you back

9

down and that little thing leapt right back onto the rim and pulled herself over. I thought she would hurt herself falling onto the ground, but she was fine. She's been following you around ever since."

"Long whiskies," I said, making the horse rock faster. My cat peeked out from beneath the bed before darting back in again.

"Whiskers," my dad said, but laughed anyway.

"Whiskey," I replied, struggling to say the name like he did.

My dad stood up and seemed to grow right in front of me. He was so tall, but I could still see his blue eyes looking down at me with pride. "I wish I could take you to school on your first day, but I've got to get to work. Money makes all your hopes and dreams come true."

I hopped off of my horse with my dad's help and followed him out into the living room. Whiskey darted after, rushing herself up one of the curtains and clinging to the top. She almost made it to the curtain rod this time. My dad followed her and fought to pull her off, even as she dug her claws into the fabric.

"Whiskers, seriously, let go. You crazy cat."

My mom came out of their bedroom. She was adjusting her glasses and smoothing her curly, unruly hair. They both were dressed for work, but so differently. My mom was in a button-up purple shirt and bell-bottom blue jeans. She usually wore a skirt that went to her ankles, but she would put that on later because her bosses insisted that was what women had to wear. My father had a one-piece overall that zipped up from waist to neck. They were the colour of the desert about Phoenix but smeared with spots of grease instead. At work, he said he just stood next to a large machine that helped make parts for planes. My mom was a secretary at a cookie baking company. She was clean. He was smudgy. He was tall and she was short, though not as short as me.

Whiskey ran between my legs and back into my bedroom. My dad picked me up and swung me above his head, "All right, you're the airplane! Take-off! Time to fly to your grandma's house. She'll probably be the one to take you to school on your first day. You are getting so big!"

He kissed me on the cheek and then blew on it to make a funny sound. I laughed, and my mom attempted to reach up to me as I soared through the air. I waved at her as my dad glided me down towards her.

She said, "I can't believe you're packing his schoolbag already. And besides, I'll be taking him. I've got the day off."

My airplane ride suddenly halted but my head kept spinning. I giggled at the sensation. My dad was still holding me in his arms.

"You took the day off?" my dad said, his bottom lip pouting. "I didn't know about this."

My mom shrugged at the sudden stillness in the air. My head stopped spinning and I looked up at my dad. He was staring at my mom.

"Maybe I wanted to take the day off, too, Ruthann."

"Maybe you should, Dean, but I did it first. Guess I love him more."

My dad's mouth dropped open, "Maybe I will. And maybe you don't."

I was set down as my dad approached my mom slowly. They stared each other down before turning to me, roaring with laughter.

"Who loves him more?!" they said together, and started to come towards me.

I squealed and tried to run away. I was tired because we were up so early, but I knew I could sleep in the car as my parents battled their way through the traffic on the highways of Phoenix, Arizona. They chased me to the ground and smothered me with kisses and tickles. I laughed.

After I cuddled with Whiskey and argued with my parents about bringing her to grandma's house, I said goodbye to her as my dad picked me up and took me out to the car. Whiskey was already at the window meowing at me. I waved and snuggled against my dad's neck. He was warm, but he was always warm in the heat of Arizona. He'd be driving. My dad would be a different person behind the wheel. His eyes would go wild. I could tell when he'd turn around to see if people were behind him. They'd become redder than they were white. His eyes would dart around. His hands would tap the steering wheel. His legs would tap against the seat. He'd hit the brakes or accelerator

11

suddenly, and I'd wake up if I were asleep, or I'd be thrown around like I was on a roller coaster I'd seen on TV. Either way, we would laugh. Sometimes. He never let mom drive. She always said she preferred the bicycle and would tease my dad that he was calmer when he drove.

My mom came out with my brother in her arms. He was crying from being woken up.

My dad poked his pudgy belly and kissed his forehead, "We need to get him to my parents' place quick. The car's air conditioning is still broken." That meant the interior of the car would be too hot in only a few minutes.

She placed Christopher in the baby seat that used to be mine and as I was buckled in next to him, I wiggled his foot. He settled down when he saw me and reached out a small hand.

"You're so good with him," said my mom. "He's lucky to have a big brother to take care of him."

I nodded, even though sometimes I felt unlucky when I helped mom or dad change his diaper. For such a cute baby, he didn't do cute poos.

I sniffed carefully.

"Don't worry, Michael," my mom said. "I already changed the little monster."

I struggled against the buckle and pretended to be a dinosaur and nibble at his hand. He laughed loudly. His face was bright red, but not from finding me hilarious. It was already very warm in the car.

Arizona was hot all year round. It was mostly a desert, my dad said. During the summer, it was so dry everything felt crisp, especially your lips. Sometimes it was so hot it stung your eyes. During the winter, it wasn't so bad, but it was still warm. At night in winter, the temperature dropped but still not everyone dressed in warmer clothes. They didn't need to. My dad was not bothered by the cold, but he disliked the heat. When it was chilly, I would grab a blanket and Whiskey and I would huddle up together.

"Christopher is getting red already," my mom said to my dad.

"Don't worry, little guy, I hate the heat, too," my dad called back as he got into the driver's seat.

As soon as we settled, my dad reversed out of the driveway. His long arm reached over to steady himself over the back of my mom's seat. I looked up at him to make eye contact as he looked back to make sure it was safe to reverse out into the street, but I sunk into the back of my seat. His eyes quickly became different. Wild. Crazy. A lit cigarette hung from his lips and I crinkled my nose as the smoke stung my nostrils. Ash fluttered down into the floor of the car and I watched it disappear into the thin carpet somewhere beneath my dangling feet.

"Hi," I said to him and he looked down at me. I wanted those wild eyes to go away. His eyes softened. I could tell. Some wrinkles he made around his eyes when he wasn't happy disappeared and he winked down at me before he returned to his wild eyes. I leaned my head back against the backseat and stared up at the ceiling of the car. I wished I could look through the back window like he was trying to do so I could help him. The car moved slowly backwards out the driveway.

I tried looking out the side window but could only see the tops of each cactus and house that passed by. Cactus grew between houses and out in the desert. Some of them bloomed with pink balls that I'd always want to feel, but you didn't touch cacti. They had long thorns that could hurt you. A huge patch grew in front of my grandma's house on either side of the driveway that led to her garage and front door.

My dad helped me out of the car this time when we finally arrived at my grandma's house. He called out to the tall smiling woman standing at her front door, "Hey, Mom!"

She held out her arms and I ran for it. She swooped me up and gave me a cuddle and a kiss before giving my dad one, too.

Coming up behind us was my mom carrying Christopher. He was redder in the face. I wished he liked the heat, so he'd be happier. My parents always had to find ways to keep him cool. They'd cover him with a blanket or wipe his face with water. Mostly, they made sure he was never in the sun for too long.

13

I made a face at him to make him laugh. It worked. I couldn't carry him yet like my mom was because I wasn't big enough. I had to be sitting down and he would nestle in my arms. I'd sing to him, "Mary had a little lamb, little lamb…"

If I wasn't singing, I'd tell him about my favourite superhero, Superman, and our dad's favourite superhero, Batman. My dad would teach me how to read from all the comics he owned. I only knew a few words. I recognised all the superhero names and some simple words. I hoped to read the comics to my brother.

"Are you Batman?" I asked my dad one day.

We were snuggled on the couch. His strong arms were around me. My mom would sometimes take a photo of us with her little camera.

"I wish," my dad said. "You know how rich he is? Man, to be living in his mansion."

"Are you him? He's funny." I asked, pointing to a picture of a white-faced man with red lips.

My dad laughed. "No way. He's the Joker. He does bad things and hurts a lot of people. And yes, sometimes he's funny, but Batman needs to stop him from hurting people. In fact, Batman wants to help him get better."

"Are you him?" I asked again, this time pointing to a man with a half ugly face.

"What are you trying to say? Your dad is ugly?" He chuckled. "And no way, that's Two Face. Sometimes he's good. He'll want to do good things. He will try so hard to be the man he wants to be, but he's sick in the head. So, sometimes, he's bad. He will hurt people, even the ones he cares about the most. All depends on the flip of a coin."

"You're Batman," I decided, and snuggled into him.

"Okay. I'm Batman." He sighed and kissed the back of my head. He deepened his voice, "Batman is telling you to learn how to read."

"Will I read like you? I want to read to Christopher."

"Your brother would love that. I see you trying sometimes. You'll get better. You will," my dad said. "School will teach you. That's why it's important that you go. I didn't finish school, but I should have. I didn't care about school like I should have. I just wanted to hang out and do drugs. I shouldn't have because school will make you smart. It will make you happy. It helps you get a job so you can earn money, and all your hopes and dreams will come true."

The evening before my first day of school, I was swimming in our pool with my dad. I was trying to drown him. It wasn't working. I kept getting thrown over his shoulder with a large splash. I had to hold on to my laughter or I would be the one drowning.

I spluttered back up to the surface. My dad had a look of concern for a few seconds before I paddled over to him.

"You okay?" he said.

I nodded. I loved the pool. I couldn't remember a time when I wasn't swimming.

My dad looked sad for a moment and I touched his face. His blue eyes looked down at me.

"You nearly drowned in this pool."

"But I can swim!" I said. I couldn't remember drowning. I always thought I could swim.

"You can. You basically taught yourself. We had the sliding door open. So many little mistakes. You were in that little walker with wheels. You remember? The baby walker? You'd zoom around the house in it."

"Like Superman?"

My dad picked me up out of the water and gently splashed me back down again. "Yes. Like Superman. Well, my little hero, you decided to fly right out the back door. We had only looked away for a moment."

"Zoom!"

"Yes. Super speed. We turned around to find you gone. You weren't anywhere in the house. We looked everywhere and I saw it first. The sliding door was open and I panicked. I was so scared. I had left it open to have a cigarette. Just for a few minutes. Your mom saw it next and she rushed out. I heard her scream. I ran past her to rescue you."

My dad's blue eyes were even more like the ocean as they filled with tears. I had been to the ocean when we went to Disneyland. We'd always look at the pictures in our photo album. He held me tight to his hairy chest and I tried to squirm out of his embrace to see if he was okay.

"Your walker was upside down in the pool. I thought my little mistake had killed you. I was so scared."

He looked off into the distance.

"But I'm Superman?"

My dad let me go and laughed out loud, "You were definitely a superhero that day. We found you face down. I thought that was it. You'd held your breath the whole time. I quickly pulled you out. I think my grabbing you frightened you more than falling into the pool."

"I can swim now."

"We made sure of it," my dad said. "I taught you, but you were a natural. A fish. A little mermaid."

"A fish?" I squished my nose. "Can Superman swim?"

My dad laughed and threw me away from him and shouted, "I don't know. Can he?"

My laugh sank beneath the water.

When I resurfaced, my mom was standing at the sliding glass door. She seemed flustered, and I assumed it was from her bike ride but the sun wasn't down. She was home early. My dad was getting out of the pool. I paddled to the stairs and followed him. We both dried off quickly in the hot sun, which was barely near the horizon.

"I quit," my mom said to my dad.

My dad sighed. "You did what?"

"I'm not going back to that job," she said, her arms open to him, beckoning for a hug. She was biting her bottom lip.

I didn't know what she meant but my dad seemed to understand. He began to pace and his eyes turned wild. Was he going to go driving?

"Michael starts school tomorrow."

My dad turned to look at me and I sunk back to the top stair of the pool and sat in the water. I must have done something wrong. My name had been mentioned and his wild eyes were looking at me.

"Dean," my mom said, biting back tears, "I couldn't handle them any longer. Whistling at me. Commenting on my clothes. Eyeing me. Patting my …"

My mom looked like she wanted to say more but she glanced over at me and fell silent. I hesitated at the stares, wondering if I was in trouble or if Mom's work was instead.

My dad nodded, but continued pacing. "You should have left ages ago. We can manage. I can manage. I can do this. I never liked you biking it on the freeway anyways." He was shouting now.

I slowly stood back up onto the walkway beside the pool. My dad's eyes seemed to be calming down. Sometimes he got loud like this. Sometimes he'd slam doors on his way out to have a cigarette or hop on his motorbike and speed away. Sometimes he'd even strap the helmet on me and we'd just sit together in the driveway while he smoked and I pretended to drive the big, loud bicycle. He'd talk to

17

himself. He'd hug me. He'd tell me that he hoped I'd have a better life than he did, and that all my hopes and dreams would come true.

After awhile I said, "I'm getting cold," as the sun dipped below the horizon after all the silence and pacing. My voice seemed to wake them both up and my mom rushed over to me. On her way, she grabbed a towel and wrapped it around me.

"School tomorrow. Your first day."

My dad lit a cigarette in the background. He sucked in as much smoke as possible and blew it out before saying, "Wish I was taking you, Michael. I've got to work though. Now more than ever."

After I ate and was ready for bed, I found my dad out back smoking, staring into the pool as if it were far, far away. I walked up to him and whispered, "Goodnight, Batman."

My dad chuckled and hugged me. His eyes still stared into the water as he pulled me close. "Good night, my little hero. I love you."

My mom helped me into bed. Whiskey was already there sitting next to the pillow, watching me. As I crawled beneath the covers, her front paws would knead the mattress before she would jump up into my chest after I lay down. My mom kissed me goodnight and scratched Whiskey's chin before turning off the lights. Whiskey was already purring as she lay on my chest. I pulled her up to my neck and hugged her. She protested a little before nudging her head against my neck and falling asleep. Her breath tickled my neck and her purring and her little tiny snores soothed me to sleep.

My First First Day

The next morning I woke up to my mom pulling back the blankets. Whiskey was still hugging my neck with her front paws on either side of my neck. She meowed at my mom and growled a bit. I joined her and tried to reach for the blankets.

"I don't think so," she laughed and began to sing, "The bright sun comes up. The dew goes away."

Her voice went really high. "'Good morning! Good morning!' the little birds say.'"

And if I wasn't out of bed before the birds started to sing, she'd pull my legs until I was in her arms to receive tickles and kisses. Whiskey would sometimes go flying and sit up on the pillows and glare down the bed at us both before darting away for food and water.

"First day of school," she whispered.

I smiled and followed her slowly out into the kitchen. My brother was already in his high chair babbling over his breakfast waiting for my mom to help him finish. His little hands were reaching down towards the bowl of baby food. He saw me and flapped his fingers saying hello. Whiskey zipped out of the kitchen and into the bathroom. My mom rolled her eyes and followed.

"You have a bowl of fresh water, Whiskers, and still you try and drink out of the toilet," she said, shooing my cat back out and closing the bathroom door. My mom would put the lid down sometimes but my dad liked it up so she just closed the door instead.

My brother smacked me to get back my attention.

I kissed his cheek and he slammed his hands over and over again against the seat's tray with glee. I dodged the splatter of mashed carrots and peas and asked mom where dad was.

She sighed. "He got a ride from someone at work, so I can have the car to take you to school."

"Whiskey is ready," I said.

"No," she said, cleaning up Christopher.

"Whiskey isn't coming?"

"Cats don't go to school. Don't be silly."

I gasped. I didn't think about that at all. School was supposed to be fun. How was I going to have fun without Whiskey?

I looked at my brother in relief. "He's coming."

"No, sweetie, he's too young."

I put both of my arms up in the air with exasperation, "Who comes with me?"

"No one, Michael, just you." My mom laughed but I didn't know what was so funny. I was about to slip into serious crisis.

"All by myself? Me?" I said, realising we should have all had a bigger discussion about this school business. I now had serious doubts and questions.

My mom laughed again and it was starting to annoy me. If I knew how to lecture her about being serious I would have. Instead, I folded my arms and pouted. Sometimes this made me get what I wanted.

"You'll have your teacher and meet heaps of other kids your age. Charity will be there."

I unfolded my arms and crinkled my nose. Charity was a girl who lived near my Grandma Stoneburner's house. My grandparents lived in Phoenix too and we'd go over there often to eat food, listen to them play music and listen to them talk a lot with each other. Charity liked to hang out with me and when she found out I was at my grandparent's house, she'd ask if I could come out and play. They lived down an alcove off of the main highways of Phoenix. Kids were always playing on the sidewalk and street. They always talked about me getting married to Charity and I didn't like it.

"Don't be like that," my mom laughed, "Her parents told me it's a good school. You might even be in her class!"

My nose couldn't crinkle anymore but I tried anyway. Charity kept kissing me and telling me we were married, which made my family tease me more. Her mom and my mom would always laugh about how blonde hair and blue eyes were all the girls' weakness. I had eyes like my dad. My nose was like my mom, even when crinkled. My hair wasn't blonde anymore though. I'd stop being blonde that summer when my dad shaved my hair all off. It was starting to grow back darker and brown like my mom and dad. They kept telling me they missed my blonde hair.

"Stop it," my mom continued, "You like Charity. Come on. You were excited about school. It'll be fun. You'll love it. They'll love you."

I looked at my brother. I was tempted to fold my arms again but I didn't. I remembered I would learn to read comics and help my brother to read. I would find my hopes and my dreams. If I found them, my dad might be happy again.

But without Whiskey, it might be harder than I thought. Maybe I could teach her how to read, too, and then they'd let her come with me to school.

Phoenix, Arizona was an amazing dream. Sometimes I would see brown and yellow flat land that held small to tall cacti. Then buildings would suddenly sprout out of nowhere. The desert would turn into steel and glass. There would be cars and people everywhere. I'd see a few trees and bushes but they were only a light green or sometimes already baked by the sun. All the way to my first day of school, I asked my mom a million questions.

"Is the teacher nice? Will I eat? Why can't Whiskey come? Is your work far?"

I'd repeat the questions but I always got the same answers. She'd tell me how great the school was going to be that by the time we were closer, I imagined a beautiful oasis. The school became this place

21

surrounded by green grass. Water rose from somewhere deep within the earth into a glorious fountain that gushed hopes and dreams. Golden bricks led to the doorway of this school. I was excited and eager now.

"Are you sure Christopher can't come?" I whined as I wiggled his toes. I couldn't wait to tell him and Whiskey all about school when I got home.

But the sands of broken dreams whirled in front of me as my mom pulled up into the school's parking lot. I didn't see any fountain. I didn't see green grass, and I certainly didn't see any golden bricks. But it was still bright and exciting.

The building I was walking towards was made of white stone that when I touched it it felt like the sand that spread across the state. All the houses seemed to be made from this stone and even some of the tall buildings. I decided all buildings were made of sand because that's all they could find in Phoenix.

"This is your new school," Mom said to me as she led me by the left hand, Christopher was nestled in her left arm covered by a thin blanket, "Don't worry, school is a wonderful place where you will learn lots of wonderful things. I promise."

My mouth hung open at how large the building seemed to be. It stretched for a hundred years forever. My eyes squinted at the blazing white. The path sizzled in welcoming with each step I took. Cacti lined the sidewalk leading to the entrance. They weren't golden bricks but each of them seemed to open their arms to me. They twisted and bowed. I bowed back.

"What are you doing?" my mom said.

I babbled about the cactus, but she shook her head. "Such an imagination."

I was ready for this thing called school. I was ready for my Mondays through Fridays to be taken up with this glorious place full of hopes and dreams and toys and friends. Who wanted Saturdays and Sundays when you could spend your days in this place? I looked up at my mom and back at all the people. No. I needed my Saturdays. Cartoons in my underwear? Yes. Comics with my dad and brother? Yes. Let's not exaggerate too much with this whole school is wonderful thing.

The days turned to weeks. The weeks turned to months. The air conditioner in the car never got fixed. Dad spent longer and longer at work. My mom said he was trying to find any extra hours he could. I didn't understand. There were only twenty-four hours in a day. I learnt that from school. How could anyone find more hours? But he somehow found them. I just never saw him. When he came home, I was sleeping. Sometimes, I'd wake up to see him at my bedroom door whispering goodnight. His comic books gathered dust and he stopped buying new ones. The loud motorbike disappeared. My mom said they sold it. Her bicycle disappeared too. We would eat more at my grandparents' house. I didn't mind. It just meant more music, food and cuddles from Grandma Stoneburner.

One evening, my mom hung up the phone and unwrapped herself from its long cord. She smiled at me and hugged me, "I got a new job, Michael. We'll be okay. We'll be okay!"

I didn't know what she meant except that after my mom started to work again, my brother and I were babysat by older cousins. Sometimes, the only person who wished me goodnight was Whiskey. She'd have each of her front paws on either side of my neck as if she were hugging me tight and purr me to sleep.

"Whiskey," I said to her, "I miss Mom and Dad."

I learnt my alphabet quickly. There was even a song for it, and I'd sing it to Christopher and Whiskey. Christopher often sang with me even though he didn't sound good at all. Whiskey never tried.

Soon, I was able to both say the alphabet and sound out some words when I tried to read the old comics to my brother or Little Golden

Books. My dad didn't touch some of them for so long that dust was starting to cover his comics. Some of them I couldn't touch without my dad, but I could tell Christopher the stories, mostly from memory. I was excited when I could understand some of the words. My brother listened, his hands touching my lips as they moved. We'd both laugh.

One day after school, Dad was there waiting. He was standing out the front, as tall as the cactus next to him. His eyes were wild. A burning cigarette hung from his lips, but I still ran to him. I jumped into his arms, but I just slid right off him. He said a bad word as he lost his cigarette and then he picked me up as he stomped it out.

"Dad!" I squealed in excitement, even though I was worried. "You don't have to find your hours!"

I was getting used to my Grandma Stoneburner or my mom picking me up from school. This was a good surprise.

He had no idea what I was saying but he held my hand as we started to walk to the car. My teacher had taken us out front for those waiting to get picked up. She walked up to both of us as he stood just outside of the car along the drop off and pick up area.

"You must be Michael's father. I'm Mrs. Walker, Michael's teacher. I hear so much about you at Show and Tell. He says you're Batman, that you're his hero."

My dad ran his hand through his hair, "He's the hero. Not me. I've been working so much he's pretty much had to take care of himself. His mom started working too. Not much, but it's something."

"I just wanted to tell you Michael is doing so well. He's ahead of the other kids. I almost can't keep up with him. He just loves learning to read and he can recognise more words than anyone."

24

My dad's eyes were still wild, but he grinned down at me. I wanted the ocean in his eyes to calm down. His teeth flashed at me. I had done something wonderful.

"I can read?"

My teacher and dad nodded together. We were at the car now. He shook her hand and thanked her. She started talking to him about the classroom size and how it would be increasing as they didn't have enough teachers. I tuned her out. I couldn't wait to get home and tell Whiskey and Christopher that I could read.

My dad thanked my teacher as he strapped me into the car seat. He hopped in and we drove away. He was shaking. His eyes darted around. He struggled to light a new cigarette as the car whipped through the streets. I began to talk about learning to read and how I was the only one in class who used my left hand to hold my pencil. I told him that I had been reading the comics to Christopher and Whiskey. I rambled on about how sometimes I woke up to him wishing me good night, but my story stopped short when his hands slammed on the steering wheel.

"Michael, shut up!" his voice suddenly boomed.

I sunk into my seat and fell quiet. My ears were ringing. My dad quickly apologised, but I stayed silent the rest of the way home.

He lifted me out of the car quickly when we arrived home. I wasn't all the way out of the car strap before he started pulling hard and my torso got caught up in it. I gasped as the strap rubbed harshly against my skin. Dad plopped me onto the driveway as he slammed the car door and stomped off towards the house. I watched him go inside. The door stayed open for me and I followed slowly. My ribs hurt where the strap had caught me.

My mom wasn't home. Christopher wasn't even there. I picked up Whiskey and carried her by the mid-section to my dad standing out back looking into the pool. Whiskey meowed, trying to tell me she was uncomfortable, but I carried her out with me anyway.

"Where's Mom?" I asked.

"She's still at work. Don't worry about it," he said, lighting up a new cigarette.

"Where's Christopher?"

"He's at your grandparents' house," he said, pushing a finger against his temple and rubbing it. He motioned me inside and followed, closing the sliding glass door behind him.

"Are they coming home?" I asked as Whiskey managed to escape my clutches and run into the bedroom.

He knelt down and hugged me and told me again not to worry. He walked out into the kitchen and pulled out a bottle from the fridge. He twisted the cap and took a long drink.

"Can I have some?" I asked.

He laughed and it made me feel better. "What? This? Oh. No. This isn't for children."

He walked out of the kitchen and headed into the living room. I stared at the fridge and then at the sink. I was still thirsty even if that drink wasn't for me.

Dad was there to pick me up every day after school. He was even home when I woke up, but he never got out of bed. My mom would drop me off at school. My dad would pick me up. In the morning, I sang songs and laughed with my mom. After school, I'd sit in silence with my dad.

Every night I would ask where Mom was and if Christopher was coming home. Sometimes my brother stayed the night at my grandparents' house. Now it was Mom instead of Dad who would stand in the doorway late when she thought I was asleep and wish me

26

good night. I missed the nights when we were all home together. We'd play in the pool or play games together. We'd sing and eat together. We'd go over to Grandma and Grandpa Stoneburner's house together. The house was just quiet now.

One night when I went to kiss him good night, my dad hugged me tight for an especially long time. His breath smelled like his drink. It never smelled that bad before. Usually he left me alone but this time he wanted me near him. His hug was so long that I didn't want to hug anymore. It felt different. Tighter. Empty. He told me not to worry any more. The smell of his cigarette hugged me, too. I couldn't remember the last time he smoked in the house. He ruffled my hair and turned me around and led me towards my bedroom.

"Go to bed. Whiskers is waiting for you, I'm sure."

I turned to him and for a moment his smile had gone again. His eyes faded somewhere as they often did now. When he noticed I was looking at him, he shook his head and smiled. "Good night, my little hero, I love you."

And that was the last time my dad would say he loved me for a very long time.

You Need To Take Care Of Me

One day when I finished school, I found my grandma waiting outside the classroom to pick me up. She was tall just like my dad but with long black wavy hair. The family called her Betty Boop because her first name was Betty and she looked a little like the cartoon character. I was so excited. I ran to her and hugged her. She had the best hugs. She was so soft and warm.

"You're coming home with me today," my grandma smiled softly.

I smiled back but hugged her again. I tried to drag her into the room to show her everything, but she only laughed and waved goodbye to the teacher, who quickly nodded and turned back to all the other kids she was trying to get to pack up.

In the car, we sang songs until we pulled into the street that led to her house. She fell silent as her driveway appeared. I tried to peek up and out at what she was seeing but couldn't.

"I'm going to park on the street. You go straight into the house when we get out. Okay, Michael?"

"Okay, Grandma."

The street came off the highway like an arm of a cactus and grew out and up along the background of the Arizona desert. My grandparents lived near the end of the street where the road ended in a loop that turned back around to head back to the highway. I was used to all the cars in their driveway and having to park along the street. The Stoneburner family was a large family. I wasn't worried until the car stopped and I could hear loud voices.

I could hear shouting as soon as the car stopped and grandma opened her door. My head shot up like Whiskey's did when she wanted to hear something. If my ears could swivel like hers did, I would do so too. Instead, I turned my head to the side and listened.

I knew the voices.

My grandma helped me out of the car. Her eyes avoided mine. I just wanted to know if everything was okay. She didn't say a word, but

29

held my hand and lead me up the sidewalk towards her house. The sidewalk was still hot and everything was still bright from the afternoon sun. All the houses looked the same to me except for the large patch of cacti that grew in front of my grandparent's house. I could see where the shouting was coming from.

My hand tightened at the same time my grandmother's hand tightened. My parents were at the end of the walkway leading up to my grandparent's house but they weren't waiting for me. They were screaming at each other. I felt my heart start to beat in my throat. My stomach started hurting. I looked up at my grandma, but she was looking away at all the other houses in the street. She began to try and pull me behind her as we approached.

A voice called out to my grandmother from their front door. It was my grandpa.

"You need to handle that loudmouth woman!" he said before he went inside, slamming the door.

"Grandma, what's wrong?"

She didn't answer, but rushed me along the walkway towards the house. I didn't want to go inside. Grandpa was being just as scary as my parents. Who was the loudmouth woman, and why was she upsetting everyone?

We passed my mom and dad. They didn't see me. They were too busy yelling at each other. My dad was towering over her. His eyes glared down at her as his face glowed red. My mom was glaring up at him with her own wild eyes. Her hands in fists. I had never before heard her be so loud.

"Why do we always have to come here?" she screamed up at him. "Let's just go home! They're not going to help! We can figure it out ourselves!"

"Get in the house, Ruthann!" he screamed back. "Get out of my face!"

I didn't know what was going on but I didn't like it. My grandma scooped me up in her arms and carried me up the driveway to her door. I could see my parents still screaming but I didn't understand what they were saying.

My father suddenly seemed to explode. Even my grandma flinched as his voice echoed above the houses. My ears just heard a loud roar and his hands flew towards my mom and pushed her. She flew backwards. Her feet scrambled to stay on the ground, but she couldn't. She fell straight into the cacti that bordered the driveway.

I couldn't see any more. My eyes were closed and all I heard was my mom and I screaming together. I felt my grandma place me on the ground and push me towards the front door for a bit before her hands disappeared. The world blurred around me. Everyone was yelling and screaming and running and pushing me aside.

I don't remember how I got there but I was in the bathroom sitting on the toilet lid. My mom was in the bath. She was moaning as my grandma gently help remove the spines from the cactus bushes. That is what was so dangerous about those big cacti. They had tons of needles sticking out of them. I blinked, and the water was running and filling the bath up.

"You'll need to soak. The hot water will help," my grandma said.

My mom's eyes rolled back in her head before they focused on me and she tried to smile.

I tried to smile back but my tears gave away my terror. She stopped smiling as the water covered her and soaked the towel that lay over her.

She moaned again.

My grandma sighed. "When they get like that, it's best to go quiet. They get over it and when they do, that's when you set them straight. I once chased Conrad through the house with a frying pan. It didn't help."

My mom laughed a little, but it hurt her, and she cried out instead.

"Just soak," my grandma soothed as she left the bathroom. When she opened the bathroom door, I heard my dad and grandpa talking loudly. I didn't listen. I was too worried about my mom.

I slid off the toilet and tiptoed over to her.

"Oh, Michael, don't cry." She winced, touching my face with a wet, shaky hand, "I'll be okay. Your father is just stressed. We all are. You'll just have to help take care of me."

I repeated those words in my head. I had to take care of her. I repeated it a few more times.

"Michael?" my mom said, touching my face again, "Go play? Mommy needs some privacy."

I turned away from her and started to walk towards the door, but I saw a small washcloth hanging by the towels, and grabbed that instead. I turned back and gave it to her.

She moaned and laughed. "You're such a good boy."

I nodded and stood near where she rested her head against the tub and patted her hair. I could see a few spines floating in the water. I started to sing her our favourite songs we always sang together on car rides. I was doing what I was supposed to do now. I was taking care of her.

"Come with me there's someone that I'd like you to meet," I sang to her and she hummed along. "…and Jesus is his name…"

Things seemed to calm down when we left the bathroom. It was quiet now. My grandpa was in the back where the family would gather and sing together. I could hear him singing but we didn't go say goodbye when we left. I wanted to see if he was okay, too. But no one was talking to each other. Christopher was now in my mom's arms. I didn't know where he was in all of this. I just knew all the adults weren't talking no matter how many questions I tried to ask.

The silence was only broken when we packed away and were leaving. My grandma kissed me on the forehead and whispered, "I'll see you tomorrow."

The car ride home was silent. I tried to sing but my mom asked me to stop. My dad hadn't stopped smoking since we got out of the bathroom. His eyes had never stayed this wild for this long. Even when he looked back and smiled at me, I could see something was wrong.

We got home. Even Christopher had stayed quiet. It was a warm night. My dad and brother were sweating. My mom hurried inside, carrying Christopher who was gazing up at her longingly. I stood at the car for a bit and watched my dad. He was staring where his motorbike had been and then stared at the house.

My mom called me softly from the door, and I reluctantly went inside.

"Bedtime, Michael," she sighed. Her skin had red spots on it where the needles had been. I reached out and touched one and she winced.

"Sorry," I said, and followed her inside to my room. As I crawled into bed, Whiskey hopped up with a few meows. She was the only one being talkative.

I curled up with her and fell asleep quickly. Later that night I woke to the sound of a loud bang. Whiskey wasn't with me. I crawled out of bed and headed towards my bedroom door. It was open just a crack. I heard another loud bang.

"Whiskey?" I whispered as I opened the door wider.

The living room flickered with light from the TV. It looked like he was sitting in a spotlight. Smoke rose from my dad's chair and I heard him cough. I smiled and walked up to him.

"Hi, Batman," I said, and touched his right arm.

His hand shot up and he jerked away from me. I stepped back and I looked into his eyes. They seemed faraway, as if he were thinking hard.

"Well, look who's here," my dad's voice slurred. "If it isn't my first born. Michael. Mike. Mikey. Mickey. You're a mouse. All quiet."

"Why are you sad?" I asked, taking a step towards him. He was holding a bottle of his adult drink. I could smell it. It didn't smell nice. It made my stomach feel sick. The cigarette he held between his lips burnt my throat.

"You know," my dad hiccupped, "my father always warned me the firstborn was a curse. He told me never to have kids. Especially the firstborn. Trouble, he said. Best get rid of him. Always was a problem. You know what, my brother was a problem. He was the firstborn. But that's okay. He's got it good now. Nice family. Nice house. He has it all. You know what he said when I told him my work laid me off? He said I should rent out the house to pay out the mortgage. He even told me of some apartments to live in. You know what that means? It means we can't live here. We really just need a loan. But he won't help. None of them will. Will you help? Of course not. I have to take care of you, don't I? Well, who is going to take care of me?"

I didn't know what he was saying but I understood that I needed to help because I had done something wrong. "I'm sorry, Daddy. I can take care of you."

He squinted his eyes at me and leaned forward. "Of course you won't help. You can't. Curse of the firstborn. You just cost me money. You just take take take and never give. Just like my brother."

I rushed around to the front of the chair and grabbed him. I tried to squeeze him as hard as I could. Hugs always helped me, but this hug didn't last long. His arms shot up and I flew backwards onto the floor. In my head, I saw how my mom looked when she flew backwards into the cactus. I began to cry but he stood up so fast it took my breath away. He looked even taller than before. His face looked down at me in disgust and I saw it in him. I saw the scowl. I saw the mean, horrible face. It wasn't the nice dad I knew any more. He was mean, and he hurt the ones he loved. Good sometimes. Bad sometimes. It was in one of his comics.

"You're not Batman," I whispered as I stood up from the floor.

He teetered on his feet and pointed at me with his bottle.

"What you say to me, boy?"

This wasn't my dad. My dad was handsome. He had a great smile. His eyes sparkled. He laughed. He wrestled. He was fun. No. This was a different dad. He smelled. He couldn't walk properly. He had a sneer on his face and he wasn't fun at all. He hurt my mom and he hurt me. I thought of the Batman comics I used to read with my dad.

"You're Two-Face!" I yelled, and he roared like a horrible monster. I took a few more steps away from his chair but he took a step towards me. Something darted out at him from beneath the couch. It zoomed in front of his feet and confused him.

He swayed. "Crazy cat."

Whiskey then went and stood at the door to my bedroom and stared straight at me with glowing eyes. I ran after her and we both jumped into my bed and hid under the covers. She was purring and kneading the bed sheet with her front paws. She nuzzled my face and pushed her body against my neck and shoulders. My tummy was beginning to hurt again.

"You saved me, Whiskey," I shivered. "You're my Batman."

We curled up together and waited for the fiery sun to light up the shadows.

Dad took his brother's advice. We moved out of the house. Rented it out to another family who got to live there. We moved into an apartment much smaller than our house. It had a living room and a kitchen all in the same room. The front door was next to a large window even I could easily open. A large railing lead to other apartments next door before heading down a flight of stairs. My dad barely fit in the bathroom that was squeezed into two small bedrooms. My parents were in one. I was in the other with my brother. Summer hit and there was no more school. I wouldn't be going back, but I didn't know that yet. My dad went away, too. My mom tried to explain to me that he went to join the army, but I had no idea what that was. All I knew is that I was left to take care of her and Christopher. I helped feed him and change him, and I played with him when she needed to cry. I sang to them both. I did anything I could to help. Most of our songs were from Church service and Sunday School.

Until he came back. The scowl. The scratchy facial hair. Shadows under his eyes. He stood at the door and we all knew things were different. My dad was back from this place called The Army. They didn't want him. They couldn't keep him I had heard him say. He couldn't handle the boot camp. I tried to ask if it was because his feet were too big. I got them to laugh at least.

"An honourable discharge and now nothing. All that for nothing," he said to my mom as he paced back and forth in the living room. I felt sick again. I hadn't felt sick while he was away. I didn't like that the feeling was back. I found Whiskey nearby watching my dad carefully and I scooped her up into my arms. Her bottom legs swung loosely as I carried her away from my dad. She tried to escape my grip, but I held her tightly. My mom stood closer to the kitchen watching my dad almost as intently as Whiskey was doing even as I held her in my arms.

He threw his bag across the room, "I'm done. I'm done with this city. These people. This heat. This life. I'm done. We're cursed here!"

I flinched at the word 'curse'. He meant me. My bottom lip trembled. He still thought I was a curse. I didn't know what that meant but I knew it was a bad thing. It made him hate me and made him always angry at me.

"Let's leave," he snapped, grabbing my mom by the shoulders. "Let's go where it's cold during the winter and warm during the summer. Let's have a white Christmas and a green spring. Goodbye, sand. Hello, trees. Michigan! No desert there. No cactus."

I looked up, hearing the excitement in his voice. He was starting to sound like my old dad. I was also excited to get away from the cactus so that my mom couldn't be pushed into it ever again.

"No heat that cooks our baby," my dad continued, growing louder, "Let's go to where your family live. I could get to know them. Michael can get to know his other grandparents. Your mom always asks when we are going to visit."

"Dean," my mom sighed, "we can't just pick up and leave."

"Yes, we can. We have nothing here. The house is a money pit. The tenants aren't paying their rent. The bank is going to take it. We can't live here. The kids can grow up far away from this big city life. Let's do it. Right now."

My dad had not stopped moving since he'd arrived home. Even as he stood in front of my mom and shook her shoulders, his feet trembled and his face twitched. I could smell that bottle of drink on him and could see a pack of cigarettes in his shirt pocket. I stayed out of his way, and as soon as Dad let her go, Mom moved away from him, too.

My dad walked off and started to pick random objects from around the house and placed them in a pile in the living room. He was actually smiling. My mom noticed, too. I wanted to laugh as he put a couch cushion in his pile. One of my plastic toys was in this pile, too. It was a funny pile, but my dad seemed to want to start packing now.

"Okay, Dean," she said, worry etched across her face. "If that's what you really want."

My dad picked her up and twirled her around the room. He even chased me around and for a moment it was like it was before. I didn't know what Michigan meant, but I wanted to go there. It was going to bring my old dad back. I didn't like the new one.

"Hopes and dreams?" I asked.

He reached for me and my heart fluttered as I remembered that night he threw me aside. But he was so strong and so quick I couldn't stop him and he suddenly looked so happy. I saw that smile again and his blue eyes sparkled. My dad picked me up and held me out in front of him and said, "hopes and dreams, Michael!"

What Hopes and Dreams Look Like

"Adventure day!" my mom said, as she pushed me into the backseat of the moving truck, a big white vehicle with a large trailer in the back full of the things we kept after we moved out of the apartment.

My body barely fit around what was left of our house. We had emptied it into this vehicle where I became one with a big cardboard box of kitchen appliances mixed in with some unwashed clothing. My mom then pushed Whiskey in beside me, and she quickly disappeared into the contents of the compact U-Haul truck. While we were on the road she'd sometimes stick her head out from a lampshade to say hello or snuggle up to me when she was ready for a nap. Behind me was a wall with a small rear window through which we could see the trailer in the back with our wooden couch with its cushions stacked nearby. My dad's matching chair was stuffed next to it with the matching end table and its cushions. My rocking horse was back there sitting all alone. So were boxes full of Dad's comics. I wished I were back there on the horse reading some of the comics.

As we drove away from our house, Dad explained where we were going.

"Arizona is a southern border state. A border is a line marking different parts of the land. We are going to be leaving the borders of Arizona and head northeast across the borders of a few states, ending in Michigan. If you look on the map, Michigan looks like a mitten."

My dad spoke in his old voice. It was his fun voice. Even as he drove, his eyes weren't wild but excited.

"What's a mitten?" I asked.

"He doesn't know what a mitten is," my dad gasped at my mom.

"He will this winter," she said with a giggle.

"You wear mittens on your hands to keep them warm in the cold weather. I will show you when we get to Michigan."

My parents had hired a large truck that held all of our things. It had big letters on the side of it called U-Haul. My dad drove the whole way and I learnt that he couldn't drive unless a cigarette hung from his lips. It was as if no vehicle could start unless he lit a cigarette up first. I decided I didn't want to drive. It was bad for your lungs.

My mom was sitting in front with a large paper map. Her unruly curly hair bobbed around from the windows that were cracked open to let my dad's cigarette smoke out. I was more interested in the fresh air that came in. My brother was crammed into his car seat with me in the back. Some of our bags and boxes full of our belongings were with us.

"We're heading to my home town," my mom said, looking back at me from the front of the truck. "Beaverton, Michigan. You'll get to see your Grandma Boyer again. You won't remember, but we stayed with her for two weeks when you were a baby. We're going to live with her for a while until our new house is ready."

"Sooner rather than later," my dad muttered. He scratched the top of his head where his dark brown hair was refusing to fall out. It was like a little island. I told myself I would never scratch my head. It was bad for your hair.

My life was like the scenery outside of the truck. It passed by me like a blur. Only a few days earlier we had been sitting around playing music with Grandpa Stoneburner and I was watching my Grandma Stoneburner look at me quietly as her hand smacked the tambourine. I could see the sadness in her smile. After the singing we ate together and hugged. She hugged me extra tight and kissed my forehead. Her soft arms made me feel safe, and when she let me go I felt like I was floating away. They stood at the doorway of their house. Our car was gone. The motorbike never came back. We now had a borrowed the U-Haul truck that to help us move out of the apartment.

"What about school?" I asked in the tight space behind their large seats. I was sitting in the middle of my seat, squashed in by the big box and other belongings. Christopher was on the other side of the box and Whiskey was also somewhere, playing hide-and-seek with me.

"School is on break for the rest of the summer." My mom looked back at me. She smiled and passed me a snack. It was my favourite: two oatmeal cookies stuck together with cream. I took it hungrily. "You'll start at your new school after. A new day. With new friends and a new teacher."

"A new first day?" I said, raising my hands as best as I could in a shrug.

"Yes. You're lucky to start two first days of school," my mom said. "How exciting?"

I saw my brother's little hand wave in the air on the other side of the box.

"Can Christopher come this time?"

My mom laughed. I looked to see if my dad was laughing but his eyes were on the road. His lips were tightly closed around his cigarette. "No, Michael. Not for a long while. And no, Whiskey can't go either. Don't ask."

We both laughed. I liked seeing her laugh. I wanted to make my dad laugh, too.

"Maybe you can come, Dad," I said, "and read comics to everyone."

My mom looked over at my dad. I leaned forward to catch a peak at his face. Silence fell over the car before my dad blinked and looked over at my mom.

"What?" My dad sighed and returned to watching the road. "I have a long drive. I need to concentrate."

I looked out the window. I could in this truck. The seats were higher than in our car. We were almost looking down at other vehicles. We'd had a good laugh when my mom struggled as she climbed into the vehicle with her short legs. When I laughed the longest, she looked at me and asked if I wanted to try on my own. I stopped laughing. Dad had to lift me into my seat.

After many hours, the land changed outside and so did the temperature. I could tell because the truck started off with closed windows and air conditioning. The heat snuck in through the top of my dad's slightly opened window. His cigarette smoke barely slipped out. I breathed in the rest of it and would cough sometimes. My chest felt heavy. I was glad when the air conditioner turned off and the windows came down. The wind was so warm but no longer too hot. The air smelled differently, but this was after the sands and the tall, green cacti disappeared to tall, brown trees with needled leaves, green like the grass below. I had seen trees before but not as many. The green grass looked soft, but I barely got to see any properly as we travelled down the grey road and everything blurred past us. The day turned to night and back to day again before my mom started to worry about how long my dad had been awake. He wanted to drive all the way from Arizona to Michigan. I had no idea which state we were in now but we had to drive through a few in order to get to the mitten. We finally stopped at a motel next door to a gas station in the early evening.

I woke up from the stop. My dad's eyes looked red and saggy.

"I could have made it," he said, and I ducked my head down. He sounded like he was getting mad.

"I know," my mom murmured, "but doesn't a bed sound nice?"

"Beds cost money. But fine. I need cigarettes right now."

My dad got out and walked over to the gas station. We had stopped at many of those and I learned that those places fed vehicles and also fed us. We were long passed the first night and in the early hours of the second day. We also got to use the toilet. Rest stops were other areas we could go to the toilet and so could Whiskey. Sometimes she went in the truck and we had to pull over and clean it out. We laughed at the smell. It was almost as bad as my brother's dirty diapers.

My mom went into the front office of the motel. I watched her go, listening to Christopher's snores and Whiskey rummaging through a box somewhere.

My mom returned after a few minutes. "We have a problem."

I looked at her and frowned.

"This place doesn't accept pets. They won't allow Whiskers in."

I opened my eyes wide.

"Don't worry." My mom winked at me. "We will sneak her in, but she'll have to stay here in the van until it's safe. We'll lose our deposit if they find out."

I wasn't sure what a deposit was. "What's a dezit?"

My mom smiled, "A deposit is money we have to give to promise we'll take care of the room we rent. We get the deposit back if we take care of their things and obey the rules."

I nodded my head. At my old school, my teacher had taught us about sharing and taking care of other people's things. Also about obeying rules. I understood.

When my dad returned, my mom explained about Whiskey. He rubbed his hands through his hair at the side of his head and I remembered that Grandpa Stoneburner did that a lot too, but Grandpa Stoneburner was balder than my dad.

"Don't do that," I tried to warn my dad, but he didn't listen.

"We can sneak her in. We'll just wait until later."

My dad grabbed a key from my mom and went to the door to our room. My mom helped me out and then got my brother out of the car.

"Whiskey," I called, but my mom closed the door.

"No, no, Michael," she said. "She has to stay in here for a while, until it's safe."

I followed my mom and turned back towards the truck every now and then. Whiskey didn't appear at any of the windows. I wondered if she knew she had to hide.

The inside of the room was very brown and I didn't like it. It smelled old and dusty and my mom sneezed a lot. My dad smoked in the room and I wished it wasn't allowed. His smoking indoors always made my chest hurt.

My mom placed Christopher on the bed. My dad continued to pace around the room. I stayed near the window and watched the U-Haul. My stomach was also starting to hurt the longer it took for the sun to set. I kept sending silent thoughts to Whiskey hoping she'd hear like some of the superheroes could do. They could think things in their mind and make other people think them too.

"Whiskey, stay hidden," I thought. "Stay safe."

I was sure she heard me because I never saw her at the vehicle window and it wasn't until after dark when my mom went out and returned with her in her arms.

"I had to clean a few messes as quickly as I could," my mom said. "But here she is."

When Whiskey saw me she let out a loud meow and kicked my mom with her back legs as she leapt out at me. I leaned down to the floor Whiskey plopped down on and she ran between my legs and rubbed up against me. I grabbed her and pulled her up to my face and we rubbed faces together.

We played for a bit with Christopher before there was a knock at the door. My mom and dad looked wide eyed at me and I ran to the back of the room, as far away as possible from the door. My mom stood near the bed as my dad went to the door and cracked it open.

"Got reports you brought a pet into the room, sir," a deep voice growled. "I need to inspect the room or you lose your security deposit."

My dad looked back at my mom, who had scooped Christopher up into her arms. He opened the door wider. "Would it really make that much of a difference? Seriously? We're tired. Drove all the way from Phoenix, Arizona with my wife and two boys. Give us a break."

My mom whispered a warning, "Dean, please don't."

The deep voice growled again, "Policies are made for a reason. You can refuse me entry, but the deposit will be mine. A lot of money to lose."

My dad grunted and took a step towards the man. I reappeared at my mom's side and held her hand. She looked at me with a big frown but I smiled up at her.

"Stay quiet, Whiskey," I thought really hard. "Don't let the mean man find you."

Dad allowed the deep voiced man into room, and he looked around everywhere, even under the bed. He kicked the cot where I would sleep and made a sound. My mom was putting Christopher back onto the bed where he would be sleeping between my parents. I winced as the man

44

stormed past me and looked behind cupboards and tables. He walked into the bathroom and back out again, shrugging his shoulders.

"Our mistake, sir, ma'am," he said and ran his hands through his hair like my dad did. I think guys did that when they were not happy. "I'll make sure that deposit is returned to you, and please accept our complimentary coffee in the morning free of charge."

My dad stared at him, his lip curled up like the villain in Batman. I hid behind my mom, who was looking around the room with her mouth hanging open. My dad slammed the door behind the man as he left, and then looked around the room just like my mom was doing. I stood there and watched them in confusion.

"This can't be," my mom said as she started to look for Whiskey. "I mean, I thought for sure the deposit was gone."

"Where is she?" my dad chuckled, lighting a cigarette as he got on all fours and checked under the bed.

They both paused in their search and looked over at me.

"What?" I looked at my parents as if they were weird.

"Where is that cat?" my dad asked with a huge grin on his face.

"Where's Whiskers?" my mom giggled.

We heard a small meow from the back of the room and Mom and Dad both rushed past me. I followed close behind, checking on my brother on the big bed. He hadn't woken up even with the loud, mean man. My parents were now in the bathroom and I peeked in through the doorway.

A small meow startled them as they looked down at the toilet. The lid was closed but it rattled a bit.

My dad leaned back against the bathroom wall and let out a huge laugh.

My mom looked at me. "Oh my god, Michael."

She opened the toilet lid and Whiskey popped her head up and looked over at me. Her ears were flattened against her head and I knew what that meant. She was worried or angry.

45

I went into the bathroom and knelt down beside her and smiled. "It's okay, Whiskey. The mean man is gone now."

She leapt out of the toilet. She wiggled each of paws to dry them. As my mom reached down with a towel to help her dry out, Whiskey's tail flicked water up into my mom's face. My mom squealed but my dad kept roaring with laughter. He was starting to cough now because he had laughed so much. Whenever he coughed like that he was trying to be funny and say that he needed a cigarette.

My mom leaned against the bathroom sink cupboard and started laughing. Whiskey and I left them to it and returned to playing.

In the early hours of the morning, my parents snuck us all out to the van with me holding Whiskey. Once they were in their seats, Mom and Dad turned to stare at me strapped in the back with Whiskey on my lap looking blankly up at them.

"Crazy cat," my dad said.

"Crazy kid," my mom said.

My mom and dad were laughing.

I looked down at Whiskey and stroked the part of her fur on her neck that was butterscotch in colour.

"What's so funny?" I asked her. She looked up at me and meowed, pushing her face against my hand and licking my fingers lightly. She didn't know either. I could tell.

The further we drove north towards Michigan the more the trees began to appear along the road. My eyes didn't hurt like they did when I looked out over the sand back in Arizona. I was beginning to see more colours blur passed the window. I'd point and ask questions about what they were.

"They're flowers," my mom answered. "You've seen flowers before."

I had in pots or small gardens, but these flowers were growing everywhere. I wanted my dad to stop so I could play with them, but I dared not ask him to pull over. The longer we drove the more the truck had to be silent. My dad would snap at even the slightest noise, like when Whiskey played with the lampshade. I felt better when he was laughing at Whiskey and me.

At a rest stop, I rushed to a nearby grassy area before going to the bathroom. Small yellow flowers were growing everywhere. I touched one of them. They were soft. I squeezed the small petals and my fingers turned yellow.

My mom came over to me and asked what I was doing. Whiskey zoomed passed her and rolled around in the grass. My mom waited around until Whiskey went to the toilet as well. She had gone after I had went to the bathroom and came back.

"What is this?" I asked, showing her my fingers.

"Those flowers are called dandelions," she said, and leaned down next to me and picked one. She brushed it along the top of her hand. A yellow streak appeared. "You can paint yourself with them."

I squealed with excitement and picked another dandelion and smeared it on her hand. She picked another and got me on my nose.

I sneezed and then laughed.

47

"What are you two up to?" my dad said as he came back from the toilet. "We need to go."

"Flowers," I said to my dad, holding one up to him. "Painting flowers."

"Dandelions," my mom said to me.

"Dan lions," I said.

My dad sighed. "They're weeds, not flowers. Come on, we need to go. Still have a long way. Kansas will go on forever."

"Kansas?" I said. "Dorothy?"

My mom nodded with a huge grin. "Yes, Michael. That is where Dorothy is from before she goes to Oz."

I began to sing "Somewhere Over the Rainbow". My mom joined in as she took my hand and led me back to the U-Haul truck. Whiskey meowed loudly behind us and I turned to see my dad scoop her up and bring her back to the vehicle with us.

My cat landed in my lap and sniffed the top of my hand. She then shook her head roughly and sneezed.

"Dan lions," I told her.

My dad wasn't wrong. Kansas didn't seem to end. It was almost as if the trees decided to only grow in little patches and the land seemed so flat and went on for almost forever. It seemed like it to me anyway.

"Where are the leafs?" I asked.

"Leaves?" my mom said. "You mean the pine trees? They have needles, not leaves."

I had learnt the words in school and I sighed. I didn't like being wrong.

"Where are the pines?"

"Back in Colorado," my dad said, "Kansas is more flat and full of crops."

"Cops?" I asked.

"Crops. Plants. Things we eat. Corn. Carrots. Potatoes. Food."

I crinkled my nose. I hated carrots, but I kept that to myself.

"Four more states," my dad said, and we kept driving. My window finally changed from flat to towns and trees again. Everything was changing, and I liked it. It was better than from house to apartment. From one of my dad's faces to the other. I stared out of the window and sang songs quietly to myself. I imagined my Grandma Stoneburner banging her tambourine and my Grandpa Stoneburner plucking his banjo. I couldn't wait till we got to my new house and I could visit them again.

By the time we reached Michigan, the trees stood tall and majestic. I must admit I preferred them over the needled soldiers back in Arizona. The roads turned from smooth blacktop to clumpy messes of dirt and potholes. The buildings that once grew to the heavens were now replaced with random water towers and electrical lines.

"We're here," mom seemed to sigh with relief as the U-Haul truck went through a toll booth. We had to pay money to enter Michigan, something I couldn't remember if we did in the other states. I had slept through a lot. Maybe Michigan was special?

My dad's hands were shaking. His eyes were bloodshot and I was sure I could see a new patch of skin on the top of his head.

"Soon you'll see one of my favourite animals," my mom said, peering out the window of the U-Haul. "The squirrel."

The car made a sudden jump as the tires clunked over the road.

"That was one," my dad grinned.

"Dean!" my mom said, I was too busy looking out at the side of the road for this illusive squirrel. I didn't even know what they looked like.

These rough roads weren't flat like in Kansas. They weaved left and right and up and down. Sometimes the trees grew over the roads and it was like driving through a dark tunnel. I loved how green it was, and didn't miss the bright sands of Arizona. When we pulled into a rest stop, my mom warned me to watch Whiskey.

"As soon as she sees a squirrel, she'll want to chase it."

"Quirrels," I said, looking around with Whiskey. She refused to go too far from me, but even if she did all I had to do was call her name and she'd return.

"Squirrels," my mom corrected and pointed to a tree. "Quick, look. A chipmunk."

A small creature scrambled up the tree just as I looked at it. I sort of jumped and then I looked around me. I could see many creatures. It was completely different from Phoenix. There were blue birds in the trees, and brown birds with red bellies fluttering in and out of branches and settling on the ground to peck for food.

As we headed back to the vehicle, Whiskey in my arms, my mom tapped my shoulder and pointed across the road. There stood some cows behind a wired fence. I had seen cows on TV and in picture-books, even out the window on our way to Michigan, but it was amazing to see them so close. I could also see horses, further out. I wanted to go over and get closer, but I had to get back into the van with Whiskey.

"You'll see more all the time now, Michael," my mom said as we began to drive further north. "You'll see deer, rabbits and opossums. Maybe even racoons, but I hope not. I don't like them. If we go way north of where we'll be living, you could even see bears, wolverines, and wolves."

"Maybe even skunks," my dad laughed.

My mom shuddered, "Oh I hope not. Not up close, anyway."

The Feisty Mrs. Irene Boyer

After a few more rest stops, we finally pulled into a long driveway that led to a quaint house that couldn't decide if it lived in the field in front of it or the forest behind it. It looked so small to me in comparison to the tall building back in Phoenix. As we travelled through different states whose names I had already forgotten, I noticed there were fewer buildings and more trees. It was like Arizona made up for lack of trees with buildings and cacti. I liked the differences and part of me wanted to go back and tell Grandma and Grandpa Stoneburner everything that I had learnt and saw, but then we wouldn't have a home and dad wouldn't be happy anymore. His hopes and dreams started with this small house, not even two stories high. A large tree grew in the front with branches that seemed to sprout from the top and hang down all the way to the ground. I could hardly see the tree trunk through the curtain. Something about that tree, standing in front of the house near deep ditches running along the road, had my attention. It seemed so large in comparison to the house it guarded. It was simple. A large garage greeted us as we arrived that connected to the house like a right arm. I could see a small window facing the large tree where see through curtains draped partly opened. The house was pale in comparison to the blue sky. It was like a cloud against the large green yard surrounding it. There was more yard than house. Within the days of travel, my mom had told of stories of her growing up with three brothers and an adopted sister.

My mom stepped out and pulled me from the crammed van. She made a popping sound from her mouth and I giggled. Christopher was in her other arm looking tired. Whiskers sat where I had just left and sniffed the air cautiously. Her whiskers twitched with the breeze and she looked over at me and meowed. I nodded my head and she jumped out of the van and followed me. She always followed me. I picked her up into my arms. My dad had wandered off down the driveway back towards the road to smoke another cigarette.

A woman stood at the open front door. I looked at her and rubbed my eyes and then looked at my mom. The woman looked a lot like my mom but older. She had the same curly hair but instead of black it was grey. They both wore similar plastic framed glasses. Their noses were even the same. The older woman had a sweet smile but with more wrinkles. Without my mom telling me, I knew who she was even though I didn't remember ever meeting her. She was my Grandma Boyer.

"Hello, little lady," the woman said, holding out her arms wide to my mom.

My dad had suddenly appeared and scooped Christopher from my mom. She was teary eyed and rushed up to my grandmother and hugged her tightly. We all stood there in front of the door as my mom and her mom rocked back and forth.

Finally, my mom broke free and nudged me forward. "This is Michael."

The woman leaned forward, peering over her glasses down at me. Her mouth scowled at first. She wasn't looking at me. She was looking at Whiskey in my arms.

"And what is that?" she asked.

"Whiskey," I held my cat out to her.

The woman stood up straight and glared over at my father. "Let me guess. You named her that."

My mom stepped in between the two. "No, her name is Whiskers."

I nodded. "Yes, Whiskey."

The woman looked down at Whiskers and crinkled her nose. I opened my eyes wide and crinkled mine. They were the same.

She peered into my eyes and smiled at me for the first time. "Hello, Michael. I'm your grandma. You wouldn't remember but we met when you were just a baby. Your mom came up here. I couldn't be there for your birth. I wasn't told till it was too late."

"Mom," my mom warned her in a tone of voice she used on me when she was getting annoyed.

My Grandma Boyer stuck her nose up in the air in defiance, "What? It's true. Just like your wedding. You told me days before after only knowing him two weeks. How was I supposed to travel all the way from Michigan to Arizona in such short notice?"

"Mom, stop," my mom sighed and tried to pull her into a hug again but my Grandma Boyer stepped closer to me.

She looked over my head towards my father, "I hope you've learnt to control that temper. Although my grandsons are more than welcome to stay here with me where it's safe."

She looked over at my mom. "Speaking of grandsons, Rowland, bring him here."

My dad cleared his throat and approached her. No one called him by his first name. He liked to be called Dean, which was his middle name. My Grandma Boyer seemed to like to break the rules.

"Dean," my dad corrected with a hiss.

"That's not your name. That's your middle name," she said, and approached my brother in Dad's arms and smiled again. "Hello, Christopher. I am your grandma. You haven't met me because your mom decided to get married far from home and have kids and never come back to Michigan to see me. I'm glad to meet you."

"You could have visited," my dad said.

My grandma glared up at him. "I could say the same about you and yours. Besides, two weeks' notice for a wedding scheduled on the same day as my son's graduation doesn't make that easy, Rowland. Besides, I was never asked and was told you were always too busy."

My dad shoved my brother into her arms and turned back to the van, lighting up a cigarette. "I'm going to move the vehicle out of the driveway."

"Why? It's fine there. Oh and don't you dare think you'll smoke in the house," my grandma called out to him and cradled Christopher to her chest.

I followed her up the rest of the driveway across the garage door to the front door where my mom was waiting with a sad, faraway look on her face. My grandma called back to me. "And you'll put that *thing* in the garage. If she is going to stay here, she might as well kill the rodents. If there's nothing worse than cats, it's mice."

Beaverton was a small town with no beavers. I looked. Apparently they were these creatures with two large teeth and a big paddle for a tail and they swam in rivers and lakes and made their homes with branches called dams. Grandma Boyer showed me pictures. I was hoping to catch one and make Whiskey and the beaver become friends. There wasn't a ton at all, but it was still fun to explore. The trees grew more often than the cacti did in Phoenix. There were birds everywhere singing different songs. The grass was so green and soothing. I spent a lot of time that summer rolling around in the grass with Whiskers. Her home rested along a road that was dirt until it reached the Willow Tree and then turned to pavement. My mom said it was because that's when the city limits started. It wasn't a city to me. Phoenix had buildings that looked like they went into the clouds to me. Not Beaverton. The town centre was on one road and surrounding it were others houses are the occasional shop. Just over 1000 people lived in the whole of Beaverton. I couldn't count that high but Phoenix had around 800,000 people in it. I definitely couldn't count that high.

My grandma's house was both in the country as well as in the town of Beaverton. The change from pavement to dirt road was the marker for the outer limits. I wondered why country people couldn't get pavement as well. Grandma Boyer told me that they had run out of pavement. When I believed her, she laughed.

"That cat really doesn't leave your side, does she?" she asked me one afternoon I was out playing in the front yard with Whiskey. She was out putting a large jar full of tea she left out for the sun to heat up. I wasn't a fan of tea but my mom kept going on and on about how much she missed it.

I shook my head.

"She thinks she's a dog, doesn't she?"

"No, Grandma, she's a cat," I giggled as I boxed with her. Whiskey loved to box. I'd sneak my hand up towards her and she'd swat it away with her front paws taking turns with each one.

"Have you tried to learn how to say Whiskers? Try it: Whisk. Ers. It's a much better name than the word you use. That word only causes trouble and violence," my Grandma Boyer said to me as she continued to watch us play.

I just giggled and asked her if she wanted to play.

"Me? With a cat? No thank you," she said indignantly, "Besides, my kind of games are inside. Here, let me show you. Come with me and bring that beast with you. I thought I heard a mouse in the garage this morning. She needs to earn her keep."

I followed her and Whiskey followed me. She was put into the garage. It was cold and had walls full of tools and other equipment I didn't recognise. My Grandpa Boyer worked in a machine shop that sounded like what my dad did and my Grandpa Stoneburner did. Grandpa Boyer was a quiet man who liked to flip his fake teeth in front of everyone and pretend they fell out.

Grandma Boyer was very different to my other grandmother.

"I am going to warn you, young man." My Grandma Boyer looked down at me with her glasses slipping to the tip of her nose. I was sitting in the living room on the couch in front of a coffee table. In front of us against the wall was a television much larger than the one we had in Arizona. They had a small one in the kitchen but even my hand was bigger than the black and white screen. The one in the living room could almost fit me into it. I looked up into her eyes. Her eyes looked so much like my mother's it made me smile. They were brown and gentle. Her words, though, sometimes didn't make me smile. They made me worry. Like now. "I'm going to warn you that I can be a feisty old coot. So you best watch yourself and mind your manners."

I had no idea what "feisty" meant but I soon found out. Feisty was someone who didn't always play nice. Adults said "feisty" as though it was a good thing, but sometimes it meant the person was unkind. I learnt that very quickly.

"There will be no shoes in the house. I see you with shoes on then you'll be the one spending the afternoon mopping the floor. You leave a mess, you clean the mess. You don't watch your tongue then I'll wash it for you."

I stuck out my tongue and looked down at it. Why did I have to watch it?

Her left hand lashed out and grabbed my face. Her fingers squashed my cheeks together. "Don't be smart with me. You know exactly what I mean, young man. There will be no bad language in this house. You say a swear word and I will wash that mouth out with soap. Do you understand me?"

I nodded my head. I understood now and I tried not to laugh at the fact I had stuck out my tongue to actually watch over it. It didn't seem like Grandma would get the joke. She let go of my face.

"There will be no roughhousing inside. You want to be a boy then you be a boy out in the yard. That's where you can play those games. In this house, there are only my kind of games allowed."

"Can girls roughhouse?"

She squashed my cheeks together again. "So, I see you'll be as smart as your dad."

I nodded quietly and half smiled.

"That's not a good thing," she said, and let go of my face. "You want to be smart in my house then you'll meet the Willow Tree. She fixes smart mouths and little brats."

"What's a Willow Tree?" I asked her.

She shook her head. "You'll find out sooner rather than later, I'm guessing."

My mom and dad were walking in and out of the house unpacking still. The U-Haul truck had to be returned and so much of our things were now in the garage where Whiskey would try to hide in a box that was being carried in. I think she was trying to sneak passed Grandma

Boyer, but she always found Whiskey and put her back into the garage. Not all of our things could be unpacked. I had my mom's old room. My parents had one of my uncle's old rooms. My room was across from the bathroom. It had bunk beds in it. I slept on the bottom and wondered who slept on the top. Grandma Boyer told me it used to my mom's and my aunt's room. I tried to suggest that Whiskey or Christopher sleep there but she explained to me, she said for the last time, that Whiskey was in the garage and besides, Christopher was in his crib in my parent's room.

The garage was down the hall too through a side door they mostly kept open. The cars were all parked outside. Sometimes the garage would be set up with a long table to fit in the whole Boyer family. For now, it was Whiskers' room and our storage.

"Your little beast will stay in the garage. I expect a lot of dead mice to show up around here. Whiskers is not to be in the house under no circumstances unless those rodents make their way in here. Also, she is not to go into the backyard as that's where the dog is, unless you want your little beast to be his supper," my grandma scolded, a chain catching her glasses as they slipped off her nose. She was towering over me.

"Whiskey sleeps with me at night," I tried to tell her, but she pointed a finger in my face.

"Whiskers," she corrected, "will follow the rules. You will follow the rules. The rules are made by me not you."

I nodded and repeated, "Feisty?"

My grandma straightened and adjusted her glasses back on her face, glowering down at me before she broke into a slight smile. I grinned up at her hopefully.

"Anyway, now that you know the rules and I know you like to play games outside, the real question is, are you good at games inside the house too?" she quickly asked me, taking her glasses off again and with her blouse.

"I like games," I said.

"I didn't ask you if you liked games, Mike, I asked you if you were good at them."

My ears twitched at the shortening of my name, but I liked the way she said it. I felt it was a feisty way of saying it, as if we were breaking a rule.

"What games?" I asked. "At school we played indoor games. Chutes and Ladders. It helps us count. I like it."

"Chutes and Ladders, you say?" she grinned, her fingers tapping together after she put her glasses back on. "I just happen to have that game, but I think your game will be Trouble. Something I suspect you'll be in a lot of."

I didn't hear the last bit she said to me because I was watching her fiddle with her glasses. She let them slide down her nose like they were going down a slide whenever she didn't seem to need them. They'd bounce and sway on their chain around her neck like a swing.

Besides, I never heard of Trouble, except when I was in it, so I didn't know how it could be a game.

She walked away from me and opened a small cupboard where I saw so many games I couldn't even count them.

"So many games!"

She pulled out three board games and placed them on the couch next to me.

I pointed to one that started with a T. "T. Tuh. Trouble?"

She sat down on the other side of the couch, raised her eyebrows and smiled. "Very good. You have impressed me. I'm not easily impressed."

"Feisty?" I said and we both giggled.

"I shouldn't have taught you that word," she said. "You learn quick. I need to watch myself."

"Like my tongue?"

She leaned back and laughed before resuming her composure. "You're a lot like your mother."

She pointed to another one of the games, "And this one?"

I looked at its letter and said, "S. Like Stoneburner?"

"Correct," she nodded. "But what's the word?"

I struggled and failed.

"This one is called Sorry," she smiled, "a word you will learn just as quickly as feisty. I expect you'll say it a lot."

I recognised the third one. It had a picture of children climbing ladders and sliding down slides.

"Chutes and Ladders!" I said.

She began opening up Trouble. It had a plastic bubble in the middle of the board game where if you pushed down on it, it popped back up and made the dice jump around. I learnt that we had to race across the board beginning in one place and finishing back all the way around where you started and into safety. I also learnt that my Grandma Boyer was very good at winning games.

My little plastic pieces were nowhere near the end when she sat back and said, "I win. You didn't do too well, did you? We'll just count this one as practice. Next time, you will owe me a penny."

I knew that a penny was a small, brown copper coin worth one cent. All the adults had pennies. Purses were full of them. Pockets were full of them. Sometimes bowls in houses were full of them. They were everywhere, and adults loved to collect them.

"So that's what pennies are for," I said quietly, as she set up the other game.

"This one is Sorry," she said. "And it's a lot like Trouble, but instead of a bubble with die, we have cards. Some of the cards have special rules. I always play Sorry after Trouble."

"When you're in trouble, you have to say you're sorry," I said.

My grandma winked at me. "That's very true. Sometimes you say you're sorry even when you don't mean it. It makes people feel better."

I nodded and thought while she shuffled the cards. They weaved in and out of her fingers and flew from one hand to another. "Like when my dad pushed my mom into the cactus?"

My grandma paused her shuffling. "I beg your pardon?"

She was looking at me over her glasses again. I sunk back into the soft cushions of the couch.

"He was upset, but my mom said sorry, but he didn't say sorry for pushing her. That was okay because when my mom said sorry, it was all okay," I said.

She held up a hand and shook her head. "Stop!"

She leaned over me again, "Let me tell you something. Another rule in this house, You will never ever hit or push anyone around. Ever. In fact, Mike, if I hear that you hit anyone…ever…then you'll meet the Willow Tree many times until you learn that it's not okay to hurt people."

I nodded quickly, and she reached her left hand towards me and ruffled my hair. She put the cards down and flipped one over and said, "Ah ha, a two. I get to move a person out and pick another card."

She picked another card, "Ah ha, a one. I get to move another person out. But this person is blocking me, so I need to move them out first. You're already losing."

I grinned and leaned over the game with excitement. She beat me at this one as well, but as I flipped over the cards we both learnt something about each other.

"You're left-handed," she grinned, "just like me."

I looked at my hand. It was left. I looked at my other hand. It was right. I looked at my left hand again.

"What?"

She tenderly raised my left hand with hers.

"We are both left-handed people. That means we use our left hand more than our right hand. We are very rare. Many creative people are left-handed. You are very special. Just like me. You know? When I was young, the nuns at school would tie my hand behind my back and try to force me to use my right. It didn't work."

"Because you're feisty?"

She howled with laughter. "You, young man, and I are going to get along."

Who Let You In?

I was born with two birthmarks. Most people, my mom told me, weren't born with birthmarks at all. Mine were a light brown. One was on my belly, where I could hide it easily. It was just a small tan dot. The other tanned spot was below my chin line on my neck. If you looked at my neck quickly, you might think it was a smudge of dirt.

My Grandma Boyer didn't know much about me. That first day we spent playing board games she asked heaps of questions. Then before dinner, she told me to wash my hands before coming to the table. I did as I was told, and when she asked to inspect my hands she was staring at my chin and neck instead. She frowned and told me to follow her into the kitchen where she grabbed a washcloth and began washing my face.

I smiled up at her and she smiled back until she began to scrub harder. Frustration spread across her face.

"What have you been up to? You've got dirt all over your face," she muttered.

I made a face. I hated getting dirty, so I was determined to let her clean my face, but it was beginning to hurt.

She scrubbed harder. "Is this oil or something?"

It felt as if my skin was going to tear off. I began to cry out and pull away from her.

My mom entered the room quickly and said, "Mom, what are you doing?"

"This stain…just…won't…go away."

"Mom!" she rushed over to me and pulled Grandma's hand away from my face. "That's his birthmark. Look at his skin! It's all red."

"Birthmark?" My Grandma Boyer frowned down at me, then gasped in horror and drew me into her arms. "I am so sorry, Michael. I'm a fool."

I tried to wipe my tears away as she smothered me with hugs, "It's okay, grandma."

She gently pushed me away and held a finger in the air. "I know what will fix you right up."

She went over to the fridge and opened the door. She pulled out a glass dish and placed it on the counter.

"Mom," my mom said, "is that pumpkin pie?"

My Grandma Boyer nodded. "Yes, I made it for dessert, but I think Michael deserves a taste right now. Don't you?"

My mom rushed up to her as if she were a little girl skipping rope. "I deserve a taste, too! Is that from the family recipe?"

My Grandma Boyer looked at her over her glasses. "Of course it is. Straight over on the Mayflower. Where else would I get the recipe?"

My mom bounced up and down, and I giggled. The pumpkin pie looked so good, and I desperately wanted a taste. I forgot all about my scrubbed neck.

"What is it?" I asked, following my mom over to the counter. The pie was smooth like glass with a brown crust growing around it. It had a brown tint to it much like my birthmark. My grandma took a knife and cut through the pie easily and placed a small slice on a plate.

"There's a tub of cream I whipped up in the fridge," she said to my mom.

Mom rushed over to the fridge and found it quickly. It was as if she had done this before, many times. I liked watching my mom and her mom together.

My grandma got out two more plates and put a slice on each. My mom already had a spoon out to scoop the cream. She put a dollop on each slice. My grandma started humming a song and my mom laughed.

"I haven't heard that in years!"

I listened as both of them starting singing together, "Found a peanut. Found a peanut! Found a peanut just now! Oh, I just now found a peanut. Found a peanut just now! Ate it anyway, ate it anyway…"

Music made people so happy. It even made me feel a burst of joy and I watched as they prepared the treat for us. They both told me to go to the table in the dining room, where we all sat and prepared to eat the dessert. By the time it was ready, I was able to sing parts of the song too.

My spoon went through the pie easily and I lifted it up to my mouth. I smelled it. It was sweet and spicy. I liked it. It almost tickled my nose.

The cream and the pie slipped into my mouth quickly and my eyes looked up at my grandma and mom who were watching me intently. My eyes rolled backwards as my mouth squished the pie together. It was so soft, and it was so delicious.

My obsession with pumpkin pie began that night. My grandma seemed proud of herself as we laughed and sang while we ate our treat. We all had finished when my dad walked in announcing he had finished unpacking.

My grandma sniffed, "Out back smoking too, it seems. That dirty habit will kill you one day," she said, as she started to gather the plates.

My dad looked at the table. "What was this?"

"Puckin Pie," I said.

My grandma walked past him. "Perhaps if you didn't waste your time with your terrible habits, you could have been in here having pumpkin pie."

My mom lowered her head as she walked passed my dad, too, following my grandma to the kitchen. I reached out to my dad for a hug, but he turned away and went back outside.

The dining room was so empty and a bit cold. It was a small, rectangular room just off the garage. Whiskey was on the other side of the door leading into the garage. I could hear her meow a hello to me. I was sad she wasn't allowed in the house.

"Sorry, Whiskey," I said quietly. "You aren't allowed. Maybe if you kill mice my grandma will let you in."

I slipped out of the chair and turned to head back into the hallway. My grandma was standing there with a small smile on her face. She tried to

65

turn it into a scowl, but I was beginning to know her tricks. She liked to pretend she was feisty, but I was beginning to learn that I could make her do something that I enjoyed making people do. I made her laugh.

That night I woke up to the door opening up a bit. Light streamed into the dark room where I slept. I opened my eyes and before I could see who it was the door closed and I was in darkness again.

Something jumped onto the foot of my bed, but I didn't need to see what it was. I could hear who it was. She was purring loudly and a tiny meow broke through the blinding darkness. A small wet tongue touched my nose as Whiskers snuggled up to my neck and licked where my birthmark was before her purrs echoed in the room.

I snuggled up to her and happily sighed, "Whiskey."

There were many days my grandma, my mom and I would play games inside. We'd also go outside and explore the woods behind the house. Whiskey would join us and follow me closely. My grandma would look down at her in disgust and tell her she was lucky she started killing mice. If Whiskey tried to dash into the house during the day Grandma would shoo her out, but somehow my cat found a way into my bed each night. Grandma Boyer would act upset with Whiskey when she discovered her in my bed each morning, but Whiskey wasn't threatened when she was chased out. Her ears weren't flat. She didn't hiss and try to box my grandma. Some morning I thought I saw a slight grin on my Grandma Boyer's face, but I always thought I was still sleepy. My grandma hated that cat. Didn't she?

My dad would go to work with my grandpa. He was a quiet man who could make his teeth flip upside down in his mouth and take them out. It made me laugh every time he did it. Grandma Boyer would scold him and scowl, but when he wasn't looking I caught her smile. She'd wink at me when she would catch me looking at her. She taught me the songs that she and my mom sang together while cooking dinner and preparing desserts.

"I found a peanut," Grandma Boyer would sing.

My mom would sing back, "I found a peanut."

They'd laugh and sing together, "I found a peanut just now."

Soon, I was able to join in. They both loved to sing and each night before bed I'd get to hear a new song as my grandma tucked me in. Sometimes my mom would join in. Other evenings she'd watch politely from the bedroom door. She'd have tears in her eyes as she watched the two of us.

I would meet the Willow Tree many days after we started living at Grandma and Grandpa Boyer's. It had long branches that would grow up and bend over to make a hidden grove around its bark. I began to sit there with Whiskers and play.

The Willow Tree was green and beautiful. but it held a dark secret that only bad boys and girls found out about. I found out the day I dropped something and swore. I didn't mean to swear. It just came out. My mom and dad said it all the time when they dropped something.

"Oh sh-" my parents would begin, and then swear.

So when I dropped a plate, helping her put away the dishes in the kitchen, I said, "Oh --"

The plate was plastic. It wouldn't have broken, but it was just something said when my parents dropped things. I didn't mean it, but my grandma was in front of me faster than a superfast superhero. She squeezed open my mouth and shoved the bar of soap she had gotten from the kitchen sink. I think it was there just for these kind of moments. She shoved it into my mouth before I could say another word and rubbed it against my tongue and teeth.

I gagged and pulled away. "Stop it!"

She shook her head and reached for me. "There are no expletives in my house, young man!"

I didn't know what expletives were, but I could guess. At that moment, though, I couldn't apologise because my teeth felt weird and my tongue wanted to leave my mouth and move away.

I spit out the taste on the floor and checked to see if my tongue went with it.

"Did you just spit on my floor?!" my grandma shrieked.

I shrunk back away from her and clapped my hand over my mouth. I didn't know what was wrong with me. First I swore, then I spit in the house. I tried to say sorry, but bits of soap were still clogging up my mouth. I burped loudly.

Grandma turned into a whirlwind. Her eyes went wide. Her eyes were looking at me, the floor and my mouth. Her hair bounced around wildly, and her glasses threatened to slide right off her nose.

"That is it!" She howled like the wind and rushed through the house. I imagined her to be like the Tasmanian Devil on Looney Tunes. She spun out of control and swept up everything in her path, me included. I was dragged out into the front yard to the willow tree and she pointed to it.

"Break off a branch!" The wind around her continued to howl, "And make sure it doesn't break easily because if it does you'll have to pick another one."

I stayed quiet. Her eyes were like my dad's when he was driving and now when he was stressed or angry, which was almost all the time. I tried to hug her. I tried to say sorry.

"Don't be feisty!" I tried to joke with her just to get her to smile and laugh. If she would only do those things, everything would be okay.

Calling her feisty seemed to upset her more and her whirlwind turned to a tornado. She picked a branch off the tree herself, and for the first time ever I was spanked.

The lash was quick and painful. My backside stung and I cried out louder than her tornado. I told her she was mean just like my dad, and that's when she stopped. The world around me fell silent but my pain was still loud. I felt her take me in her arms and hold me.

"Don't you dare call me your father," she snapped, but held me tight. "You said a very bad word."

"My mom did a bad thing, too," I cried. "And my dad pushed her in the cactus."

My grandma looked me in the eyes, but I could barely see her through the tears, "What did you say? He did what?"

I told her about not having a house, about the cactus and about the apartment. I told her how he was mean just like her, but he was mean almost all the time. I was crying now. Grandma listened intently. Her face looked so angry, but her eyes were full of tears and sadness.

She dropped the branch from her hands. It was like a whip. It fell to the ground.

"This is different," she said quietly, but I shook my head.

"It both hurts," I sobbed.

She looked down at the branch. "This is diff --"

She stopped talking. We were still outside near The Willow Tree. I looked up at her and saw this look of terror on her face. I had said

69

something to scare her and I didn't know what. I just wanted to take it back.

"I'm sorry," I said.

"For what?" she sighed, preventing her glasses from slipping off her nose as she looked down at me. "For speaking the truth? No. You aren't the one who should be apologising, Michael."

She pulled me back towards the house. We entered the small space where our shoes and coats were put away. But instead of turning left into the house, she stormed into the garage where Whiskey was sitting near the door leading into the dining room area. I watched her quietly at the door to the garage. She reached down and grabbed her by the scruff of her neck and pushed us into the house. We marched down the short hallway towards my bedroom. Whiskey was wailing all the way, but only quietly. She was like me. She knew when she might be in trouble.

I was pushed into the bedroom and Whiskers was put onto the bed. The door was closed quickly and I could hear my grandma walk away from the door, calling out for my mom. I wasn't sure where my mom had been, but apparently my Grandma Boyer found her. I could hear them yelling though I couldn't work out what they were saying. Whiskers and I knew not to leave the room. She was just glad to see me, and I was glad to see her. We both curled up in bed and fell asleep.

The Willow Tree wasn't fun anymore. I didn't play with Whiskey near it again.

That night, dinner was quiet. My mom's face was red. My grandma chewed her food angrily. My grandpa tried to chat to all of us, but no one replied. He even tried to pretend his false teeth fell out to make us laugh. It usually did. Christopher was the only one that giggled madly from his high chair. My dad wasn't there. He was outside somewhere in the dark.

After dinner, my mom and I went outside to find him. He was standing near the garage door smoking a cigarette. My mom and I stood near him, but no one said a word. I just watched the end of his cigarette turn red and then fade away. I avoided breathing in the smoke that billowed out of his nose and mouth. We three stood in the dark for

70

a while. I stared up at the stars. There were so many of them. Back in Phoenix, you could see the stars too as they hovered over the desert around the city. I don't know why but they seemed different now that we were further north. I wandered away deeper in the shadows of night, but only far enough to get a break from dad's cigarette smoke. The porch lamp was the only light in the yard but it was dim and only highlighted the area in front of the front door.

After a while, we heard the cat bowl rattle. Usually at night, it was in the garage. One of us had forgotten to take it inside. It was left where we fed Whiskers just off the pathway of the front door. My mom walked away from my dad who was watching her quietly. His teeth hissed as he pushed smoke through them. Another hiss filled the air and my mom screamed. She backed away from the front door clawing at her clothes. My dad laughed and that's when I learnt that TV wasn't always right, and skunks did not love cats. They were not like Pepé Le Pew in Looney Tunes. A flick of a tail and a putrid spray to the face, and my mom smelled worse than my brother's diaper and Whiskey's poo combined.

"Welcome home, Ruthann," my dad said. I could see him grinning.

"Dean!" my mom squealed, as she wiped frantically at her clothes and ran around to the back of the house. We both followed her. My dad was laughing the whole time. I didn't like it. My mom seemed upset. She almost sounded like when she had been pushed into the cacti. Grandma Boyer appeared at the back door of the garage. Everything soon smelled of skunk and she ordered my mom into the bathroom. I was ordered to go into my room and get ready for bed. I ignored her command and stood at my bedroom doorway and watched.

"Richard, go to the grocery store and buy as much tomato juice as you can," Grandma Boyer said to my grandpa. "Rowland, go with him."

"Tomato juice?" I asked from the doorway still.

My grandma stood outside of the bathroom door, asking my mom to pass her clothes out. She was already holding a trash bag. "Yes, tomato juice. Your mom is going to take a bath in it. It will get rid of the smell. Now I said get ready for bed."

71

I opened my eyes wide and turned to go into the bedroom where Whiskey was waiting for me on the bed. Grandma Boyer hadn't noticed she was in the room yet so I was going to enjoy it. I didn't mind having to get ready for bed anymore. The idea of taking a bath in tomato juice didn't interest me and I didn't need to take care of my mom. Grandma Boyer was doing a great job at doing that.

Michigan was weird. It made you have baths in tomato juice.

Crazy Cat

I swallowed a penny and it was all my grandma's fault.

We were playing our board games with the bowl of pennies she brought out to keep score right above the game. So far, Grandma Boyer had taken all the pennies.

"Don't give up. You'll win one day, but only if you try hard and become as good as me," she'd say and smile her feisty smile.

It had almost been a month since we moved in and I still hadn't won a game. We were playing Chutes and Ladders and I noticed she had counted wrong. Her token had skipped a chute. She was supposed to slide down. The tokens were cardboard with printed pictures of children stuck into plastic stands. My token was the little boy in the striped shirt. I thought he looked the feistiest of all the pieces. I also liked his smile. It was cheeky looking.

My eyes widened when I realised she skipped a space, but I didn't say anything. Then it was her turn again and she did not count correctly. This time she hit a ladder to climb up closer to the end.

"Hey!" I said, and her whole body shuddered in surprise. "You cheated!"

She gasped and leaned back with a hand on her chest, "Excuse me?"

I pointed at the space where she started and counted the number she had spun. My finger slammed down on the space she was supposed to land.

"Oh," my Grandma Boyer smiled slyly, "my mistake. Glad you're finally paying attention."

I eyed her suspiciously and began counting each of her turns and every time I had to correct her. Each time she gasped and apologised for her mistake.

Soon, my piece moved closer and closer to the finish. I had started to count the spaces for her and this time her token landed on a space that had a chute. She slid it down closer towards the bottom of the board, but each of my turns she'd try to trick me into landing on a space that I wasn't supposed to land on.

"You need to go to school," I said. "You can't count."

Grandma seemed pleased with herself until in the end, when I counted all the way to the last space. One hundred. The top of the board. The winning space.

The penny was mine. My first penny.

"Well done, Mike," she smiled. "But I bet you can't win again."

We played another round, but this time Grandma didn't make counting mistakes. She would spin the spinner. Sometimes fast. Sometimes slow. Her numbers seemed to be always good and her character climbed up all the ladders.

My token landed on the longest chute and I moaned loudly. I landed pretty much back at the beginning and before I could blink a hundred times, she finished.

"Well, I win again," she said, and reached towards my penny.

"Hey," I exclaimed, "that's mine!"

"What? Oh no. The winner can take from the bowl or take from the loser. So I get to take it."

I snatched the penny up into my hand and she leaped towards me and wrestled for it. She tried to tickle me, but I wasn't ticklish. She was strong for an old lady. My fingers were loosening around the penny. I had to think of something. So I hid it. In the best place I knew.

My mouth.

She pried my fingers open and found no penny and she began to wrestle me again. I gasped at the surprise attack and I gulped and swallowed hard.

My eyes widened and she sat back, reading my face. "Where is the penny, Mike?"

I lifted my left hand up to my mouth and covered it.

"Mike," she said, "where did you put the penny?!"

I pointed at my mouth.

"Mike, open your mouth!"

I did. It was empty. I knew where the penny had gone and I think she did too.

She laughed. She laughed until tears streamed down her face. She laughed so hard her whole body fell backwards into the couch. She wrapped her arms around her body. I joined her in laughing, though a few hiccups appeared.

My mom came into the room to see what we were up to, and when my grandma tried to explain my mom freaked out.

"Michael, spit it out!" she cried.

My grandma shook her head, "It's gone, little lady, and we won't see it again for a little while.

"Where will it go?" I asked.

My grandma wiped her tears away with a handkerchief. "Where all things go that you swallow. Into your tummy and out through the other end."

"You can't just swallow pennies, Michael! The only things that go in your mouth are food and water! You could have choked!" my mom said.

"I'm going to poo it out?"

My Grandma Boyer suddenly turned serious. "We don't need to get into the details, Mike. It's not polite. Now pack up the game and wash your hands for dinner."

The penny was seen again, but it was flushed away. My first win, and I lost it completely.

Grandma Boyer sang, but she didn't play an instrument. She was different from Grandma Stoneburner back in Arizona, who would have weekly jamborees where she would play the tambourine and my Grandpa Stoneburner would mostly play the banjo. Grandma Boyer was tricky and sneaky. She was playful. She was definitely feisty and stricter, but I liked it. She took care of me while my mom and dad worked and slept. When my dad was around, he was very quiet and hardly spoke. It was like he was under constant threat from the Willow Tree and needed to make sure he didn't get into trouble. He hardly ever laughed though I tried to joke with him. And it wasn't till he came home one day that I saw him smile for the first time in many weeks. My mom didn't sleep as much as my dad did. She spent time with us.

"I've found it!" my dad suddenly said to the room.

My mom, grandma and I were playing cards.

I had just told my grandma to go fish and she was eyeing me carefully, "You better not really have a three or there will be trouble."

There wouldn't really be trouble. She would always make threats, but I learnt she just did that to be scary. Other people in the family listened to her. I didn't always, and she'd just laugh and shake her head.

"I've created a monster," my grandma would always say to me.

"And what have you found?" my Grandma Boyer now said to Dad. "Your common sense?"

I knew a penny was one cent, so I wondered if dad found his money. Would we get his motorcycle back? Would we be moving to Phoenix again? I put my cards down and frowned. I didn't want to go back, even though I missed my Grandma and Grandpa Stoneburner, but I loved the trees here. I loved the different kinds of animals, except the skunks. I loved my Grandma Boyer.

"I found a house," he grinned. "We are moving out."

My Grandma Boyer looked at me quietly and started to pack away the cards. "Well, this is a private conversation. I'll excuse myself."

I watched her disappear into her bedroom and close the door. I sat there and watched the door close and heard it latch. She seemed sad and upset and I wanted to follow her and comfort her, but my dad had moved over to us with a newspaper. He had been circling things in it and using the corded phone in the kitchen.

"We can't afford to buy a house, Dean," my mom said quietly. "We've talked about this."

"Not buying. Renting," he said. "Our own place. Until we can afford to buy."

"I don't know…" my mom trailed off.

"It's not far from here. We'll still be close to your family."

I smiled. I was glad I'd still be close to Grandma Boyer.

I stopped listening and slipped away from them. I went to find Whiskey and tell her the news. She was always waiting near the door and when she saw me she got up and meow loudly. She'd rub against my legs and let me pick her up and cuddle. I stayed there till my grandma found me and told me to wash up. I helped her make dinner and we sang our songs and teased each other for cheating on games. Well, I teased her for cheating.

"I don't cheat," she winked, "I use my resources."

Grandma Boyer didn't come with us. She didn't say much about our moving out. Sometimes I saw her talking quietly to my mom, but when I came closer, they stopped talking. My mom had looked bothered by what my grandma was saying and shaking her head.

"He's quiet. He's withdrawn. He hasn't gotten help. I can't do anything with you four not here," I heard Grandma say, though she went quiet when she saw me. She was sitting with my mom in the living room.

I crawled up into her arms and she kissed my forehead, "Hello, peanut."

The house had no other houses near it like my grandparents' houses. This one was surrounded by fields and trees. It had a long dirt driveway leading up to a small, old house with a stone pillar coming out of one of the walls.

"That's the chimney," my mom explained, "The house has a fireplace. After the summer break when it starts getting wet and cold, this will be perfect to sit around and stay warm."

"And roast marshmallows," my dad added. He seemed much happier now that we were not living at Grandma Boyer's house.

I still didn't like the idea yet.

"That's when it's going to snow?" I asked.

My mom nodded and I grinned. I had never seen snow in real life before.

A small room was built around the front door. It was like the room Grandma Boyer had in her house but bigger. We could still hang up our coats and put our boots away but also fit in a few chairs if we wanted shade in the summer or to watch the snow fall without going out when it was windy. The walls were made of the same thing screen doors had. We all stood inside of it.

It was weird seeing another moving truck get loaded with all of our things again. Grandma Boyer tried to say she was glad to get her garage back but I could still see she was upset. I kept giving her a lot of hugs.

Our new house had a basement. A large room built into the ground beneath the house. Most of the stuff from the moving truck was in the basement waiting to be unpacked into the house. I didn't like that most of my things were down there, but my mom said in the next few days they'd be unpacked. She carried a box over next to my rocking horse. The box was labelled "photos".

Through the front door some of our stuff was still in boxes. The living room was large, with the fireplace at the far end.

"That will be our room," my dad pointed to the door next to the fireplace, "And the one next to us is the bathroom. We will all have to share."

My mom walked around, holding Christopher and peeked into the bathroom and nodded before moving on, "Oh, this is the kitchen."

"And way over here across the room from the fireplace is you and your brother's room," my dad said excitedly.

I smiled at my brother who was reaching for me while snuggled in my mom's arms as she followed me over to the room. He didn't turn red anymore like he did in Phoenix. He liked it much better in Michigan. I could tell.

The moving truck drove away and we spent the day unpacking. We had been living for most of the summer with my Grandma Boyer. As the season started to end, we were excited to use the fireplace. The summer nights had been too warm but now that the weather was changing and the nights were getting colder, we could use the fireplace.

My parents also talked about bonfires where they had spent time with family eating, drinking and playing music in the jamborees we used to have in Phoenix. Dad brought out his guitar. He hadn't done that since Phoenix when Grandpa Stoneburner would insist he play. He strummed a few songs he liked by Johnny Cash, a man I was told my Grandpa Stoneburner used to play with when he was younger. I smiled as I snuggled up against my mom as she was cradling Christopher. Grandma Boyer had been watching him while we made the move. We didn't take him with us until we had the last of our things from her house.

The sun disappeared and the fire continued to brighten the room. I wanted that evening to last forever, but my eyes grew sleepy as I watched the fire. It was amazing. It danced across the wood beneath it. The fire's smoke rose into a hole that led up through the house and out of its chimney above the ceiling. The fire made me feel safe and warm.

"Mike," my mom's voice woke me as she gently shook my shoulder, "Head to bed."

I had fallen asleep in front of the fire.

I followed her slowly with Whiskey following. After my brother was put into his crib and I was tucked in with Whiskers in the bed. I could see out my bedroom door my parents put out the fire and went to bed themselves.

I woke to a howl in my ear. It snapped me out of my deep sleep and I gagged. The ceiling felt like it was right in my face. My eyes had a hard time focusing and they were stinging. I tried to call out but what I thought was the ceiling went into my open mouth. I closed my eyes. I was so tired. I just wanted to sleep, and this was a weird dream. I closed my eyes and it felt as if my bed were slowly spinning.

Another howl woke me, and something swatted my face. I snapped my eyes back open. The ceiling was closer, and it scared me.

Whiskey swatted my face again and I sat up. Her howl was so loud. Once I was upright, she leapt off the bed and disappeared out the bedroom door. I could hear her feet patter against the wooden floors. She was howling like crazy. I coughed and gagged. There was smoking filling my room and my mouth. I wanted to spit it out.

I heard a voice out in the living room, "What is your problem you crazy cat — oh my God, Ruthann, get up! Ruthann, get up!"

I leapt out of bed and looked up at the smoke slowly lowering itself to me. The doorway flickered with light. Oranges and yellows and reds. I stumbled to the doorway. My head was spinning. What used to be a beautiful fire was now licking up the walls and onto the ceiling. I couldn't even see the fireplace anymore, but I did see Whiskey running back and forth between my dad and myself. She was howling up at us. She'd bolt towards the front door and jump up against it. She'd attack my dad's feet, as he rushed back into the bedroom and reappeared with my mom. She rushed across the room past me to Christopher's crib.

My head was still spinning as I stumbled out of the bedroom door, but Whiskers slammed into my legs and nipped at my ankles. Her claws slashed at my bare feet. My mind wanted to sleep but the sting of her claws snapped me to attention. I felt my mom grab my arms and we rushed out the front door. She had Christopher in her arms. My dad looked like he was rushing around like Whiskers trying to swat at the fire that no longer stayed in the fireplace. He ran to the phone attached to the wall in the large living room that seemed so much smaller with the smoke and fire. We watched from the door as he dialed a number. He was screaming into the phone. He yelled out our address and hung the phone back up.

My mom screamed, "Call my mom!"

He struggled with the phone again. He was having a hard time not coughing.

As my mom had us back out into the porch, the smoke followed. So did my dad. We wandered out into the dirt driveway, then turned around and watched. My dad looked at each of us.

81

"Don't worry," my mom sputtered. "We're safe."

My dad looked around and I knew exactly who he was looking for. I almost screamed but he bolted towards the house.

"Not all the family is safe!" he said as he disappeared back into the billow of smoke that poured out of the house. I felt sick again. My chest hurt. My throat seemed to hold my heart. I couldn't move as my mom clutched me close to her. I started to cry.

I hated myself. How could I leave Whiskers in the house? Why didn't I save her like she had saved us?

"Whiskey," I sobbed.

"Whiskey will be okay. Your dad will get her," she whispered, kissing my forehead, but her eyes never left the front door.

I had never before heard my mom say her name the way I did.

The smoke billowed suddenly, and my dad rushed out with a fighting beast in his arms. As he neared, I could see how wild my cat's eyes were. Her ears were flattened. Her pink nose was covered in soot. She was clawing at my dad's arms and I could tell he was hurting her, but he held on tightly.

When Whiskey saw me, she howled and gave one last kick before leaping out of Dad's hands, landing on the ground safely on all fours. She dashed over to me, and my mom let me go so I could pick her up.

"Oh, Whiskey," I sniffled.

We were all coughing, even my brother, and it was as if my ears were suddenly unclogged. I could hear Christopher screaming. I could hear the fire crackling away like a super large fireplace. I could hear everyone breathing. I could hear the small, scared meows of Whiskey as she trembled in my arms.

"Whiskey saved us," my dad wheezed. "She saved us."

He had never said her name like that, either. Something had changed. We all huddled around each other, as we watched the fire consume the rest of the chimney.

A car pulled carelessly up the driveway. Stones and dirt flew up everywhere as the tires squealed to control the vehicle. The car stopped, and out hopped Grandma Boyer from the passenger side. My grandpa was driving.

"Mom! Dad!" my mom sobbed.

My grandma took her in her arms and then took Christopher from her. She hugged him while she pulled me into her free arm and clutched at me.

"What happened?" she asked, looking at my dad with an odd expression on her face.

My dad coughed and pointed to me. No, he wasn't pointing at me. He was pointing at Whiskey.

"I woke up with that crazy cat howling. I have never heard her make such noise. I went out to keep her quiet when I saw the smoke and then the fire."

"Whiskey scratched at me," I sniffled, and cleared my throat.

"She was bouncing off the walls and against the doors," my mom added. My dad had his arms around her.

My grandma looked down at my cat, but this time not with disgust. She was smiling softly, "Well, Whiskey, it looks like you earned your keep, haven't you? Our little hero."

I looked down at Whiskey too. Now she was purring and trying to wash herself.

"Let's go, Mike," Grandma said. "In the car with you and that hero of yours."

I got into the backseat of the car. My brother was strapped into the car seat.

"A nice hot bath for all of you and then straight into bed," my grandma commanded.

"Whiskey too? Can she sleep in my bed?"

Grandma Boyer adjusted her glasses. "Of course. No hero sleeps in a garage."

She closed the back door where I had crawled in and then she closed the passenger door of the car as she walked passed the front window towards my parents. She seemed to be stomping towards them.

"And you," I heard her say, "were you drinking?"

I couldn't hear what my dad said, but I could see his wild eyes from the back seat. Whiskey nipped at my fingers, demanding my attention. I could hear sirens and eventually saw the lights of the fire engine. My Grandma Boyer stayed for only a moment longer to allow all the fire fighters and police get to the house before she hopped into her car and we drove off. My parents stayed and watched the fire while standing in the driveway in each other's arms.

The Triangle

And that's how we lost our third new house. It's how we lost the rest
of our things. My rocking horse, sleeping in the basement, was now
gone. The fire had eaten my toys. It was now my turn to start all over. I
didn't even get to play with them since moving from Phoenix. They
had stayed in their boxes in a corner of Grandma Boyer's garage. My
parents lost all their things back in Phoenix, but they seemed more
bothered by all the photos they had lost. The bike. The motorbikes.
Cars. Pools. House. What else would we lose?

My dad had explained that the fireplace had been faulty. As the fire
crackled inside our new home, its soot and ash rose through the
chimney. A small part of it would rest in a crack in the stone. It was so
hot that it caught fire to the inside of the walls.

Back at Grandma Boyer's house, the fighting between my grandma
and Dad got worse. He didn't like the fact that we had to move back in
with her. I didn't mind. Whiskey wasn't happy having to return to that
garage but each night the door to my room opened and someone let her
in. I tried to stay up late to see who it was but my eyes betrayed me and
closed.

My mom and I would go for many walks in the backyard. She would
tell me stories of when she was little, how she would play army men
with her uncle and brothers. She told me stories of how they'd go
exploring and pretend they were far away in a different land. I asked
her if her sister played too, but my mom shook her head and said that
was before they adopted her. It was in that backyard full of trees and
small clearings she told me they had found another new house.

"How many houses will we have?" I asked, my hands flying up in the
air.

"Too many already," she sighed.

I said, "but I love Grandma Boyer."

"I do too," she agreed, "but we need our own home. I'm not sure how
much more your dad can take."

Whiskey was following the two of us. Since the house fire, everyone now called her Whiskey like I did.

We didn't stay very long in grandma's house. My mom was right. Dad didn't like living there. I'd get scared by the loud arguments he would have with Grandma Boyer. My mom would stay silent just like I did. She'd talk quietly with dad later, but I never heard what they said.

"Coleman?" my grandma hissed at my mom the last day we ever lived with her.

"It's a nice house. Rent, with option to buy."

"We could have found you a house closer. Mike could have gone to your old school."

"It has a great yard. Surrounded by woods for the kids to play in. It's not too far."

"Far enough away from me," Grandma Boyer snapped as we prepared to leave. She was glaring at my dad who was closing the car door.

My grandma knelt down to me before I was put into the car and gave me a hug. "All right, peanut, you behave yourself and I'll visit you often. I have games to win."

I hugged her and giggled too, but I wasn't sure if I was going to see her. The last time we moved away and I hugged Grandma Stoneburner like this, I never saw her again. Even though we wouldn't live as far away, I still wondered if I ever would see Grandma Boyer again.

I was sad, as I climbed into the car. Whiskey was in a cat cage. Grandma Boyer had gotten it for her. My brother was snoring in his carseat. It wasn't like Grandpa Boyer's snoring when he fell asleep in his chair. It was more like a snort or grunt. Sometimes a snot bubble could appear. Babies could be really gross if they wanted to be. Then we drove away to our third new house and soon I'd be going to my second first day of school.

Coleman was similar in the type of shops Beaverton had but Coleman was more spread out. Houses surrounded the paved strip of road that was called Railway. It was called Railway because there was a railroad that would travel through with goods and trades. My mom explained it to me as we drove through Coleman.

Ice cream parlour. Restaurant. Clothing shop. Gift shop. Petrol station. Beyond them were side roads leading to the houses of the locals. I didn't see a grocery store but we didn't follow Railway all the way through Coleman. We turned off to another paved road and travelled quite a ways before we turned off onto a dirt road. We went from fields with a few trees to trees guarding both sides of the road. Barden Road held only a few houses. Our house was almost down towards the dead end, where the road widened into a circle so drivers could turn around. Our house was odd. It was shaped like a triangle. I had never seen a house like that before. Most houses were square, or rectangular.

We didn't need a moving van this time. We had saved some of our belongings from the fire and they were already at the next house. We had my mom's family to help us. Anything was not in the basement or near the fireplace, like our furniture, was safe. Mom's family and friends gave everything else to us.

When we got into our new house, the first thing I noticed was that the walls were slanted. We couldn't hang up pictures and my dad was so tall he couldn't stand near the walls without crouching. The house was so slanted on both sides my dad could climb up the outside of the house all the way to the top with ease. The shingles that covered the roof helped him use his shoes. I wasn't allowed to try, though. I was too little. The house did have two flat walls, but they were the front and the back.

At the rear of the house was a small door that led to the back of the driveway. The dirt driveway curved around the house in a U shape. Vines grew up the back wall of the house. There was a small shed at the edge of the driveway and the woods. Next to the shed was a big, white metal tank that held gas that helped heat the house during winter. Inside, the house felt empty, even though it was full of both our old and new things.

The backdoor opened straight off the kitchen, which was big enough to hold a dining room table. The bathroom was tucked into one of the slanted sides behind the kitchen. I didn't like the bathroom because it had a hole in the back that led to a small crawl space under the house. When I went to the toilet, I was always afraid something would crawl through the hole and grab me, maybe like a skunk. I didn't want to have to bathe in tomato juice. The toilet was to the left of the bathroom door across from the bathtub. Then there was the sink on the other side of the toilet. It was all the colour of custard except for the toilet. I asked if all toilets were white but my mom only laughed. The hole to the crawl space was twice my size and had the hot water heater nestled into it.

There was a small room straight across from the bathroom. It was so tiny that my bed and my brother's crib were cramped together. Walking through the kitchen was the living room. It had no ceiling. It just reached up to the peak of the roof. The living room took up half of the house and faced the front yard. Large windows and a sliding glass door took up most of the wall. It was so bright in the room. The living room shared a wall with the kitchen where a small alcove rested. I could fit into it if I wanted. Board games could fit into the alcove perfectly. Against that wall were also stairs that ran parallel with the A-Framed walls. The stairs led up to another room where my parents would sleep. When we spoke, our voices would echo against the tall peaked ceiling. I felt like I was in a church steeple because of the echo. I pretended I was my dad's brother back in Arizona where he was a pastor of a Baptist Church. I loved going to that church because people danced out of their seats when they wanted to praise Jesus. There was a

lot of dancing. Grandma Boyer had us go to a Methodist Church. They
didn't dance and sing in between the pews. I had trouble concentrating
in that church. I didn't understand the difference except that one
church was louder.

 Christopher and I were going to share a room downstairs across from
the bedroom. Our room was bare with my things, and I felt very
quickly what it was like to lose all my favourite toys. Christopher still
had his baby toys. Some of them were what I had as a child. I couldn't
wait till I started buying new toys. I began to wonder if this is what it
was like when my dad lost his motorcycle, when mom lost her bicycle,
and when they both lost their jobs. I imagined where my rocking horse
would have sat in this small, shared bedroom with the crooked wall. It
didn't have a window looking outside, so the room was dark during the
day and night. The light would always have to be on inside.

 I had no toys, at first. Our room had a dresser given to us by Grandma
Boyer. It had all these old stickers on it that my mom and her adopted
sister had put on it when they were children. I loved the different
smiley faces and animals on it. I'd make up stories about them. They
were my toys for a while, and I continued the tradition of adding more
stickers to it. I had a bed. It was a mattress on a thin piece of plywood.
My Grandma Boyer made sure of it. Many things that began to appear
in my room were because of Grandma Boyer.

 I stood at the large sliding door and looked out over the front yard.
The dirt road in which we came into lead deeper into the trees to the
left and back into the trees to the main highway to the right. Later we
would walk down towards the left and realise that it ended and looped
around a few houses before coming back. When cars drove passed our
house, they always kicked up dust. If they were going fast enough, we
could hear a few pebbles hit the large window. It took a few minutes to
reach the paved road that eventually led to Coleman to intersect with
the main street. The biggest local grocery store was just outside of
town and that's where all the people whose houses surrounded the
main street must have gone to shop. It was always full of the same
people.

 It still felt so small to me just as Beaverton had felt. I could still
imagine the city of Phoenix. Everything seemed the same, especially

the people. Everyone in Coleman had white skin. Phoenix had a bunch of different people, and taller buildings and many more roads. Here there seemed to be more dirt roads than paved. I loved the trees, though. Next to our A-Frame, there was a forest that looped almost all the way around us. At first, I felt so lost, even in my own yard, but more so among the trees. My mom and dad encouraged me to explore the woods.

 Across the dirt road there were two houses separated by patches of trees and large grassy yards. They seemed so big in comparison to the A-Frame. I already missed having a house with straight walls. It was weird living in a triangle.

My Second First Day Of School

Fall was coming and the green that I loved was starting to change to reds and oranges and browns. The trees looked as though they were on fire. When the wind blew, the trees' leaves would flutter away just like the feathers of a bird. It was a different kind of beautiful than the deserts of Arizona.

The school was very different, as well. That morning of my second first day my mom drove the car up a driveway that ran along the front of the school. Unlike Phoenix, there wasn't any traffic to make the journey slow, but my third new house was so far away, it seemed to take a hundred years forever just to get there.

She stopped and quickly got out of the car, and rushed over to my door to let me out. She seemed flustered and looked around frantically. The school was not as bright as the one in Phoenix. I knew that was because the sun wasn't glaring as bright. This school was made of brick not steel. It had windows decorated differently with children's pictures and other artwork. Everyone seemed to know where they were going. Even though Coleman was a much smaller town than Phoenix, I felt lost. I stood on the sidewalk holding my tin Disney lunch pail. My food was inside. Some of the other kids were carrying bags, but these kids looked much older. I couldn't remember seeing older children at the other school. I felt small, even though the city life of Phoenix was much larger. I was scared here. Back in Arizona, I had been excited.

My mom gently nudged me towards the door of the school and kissed the back of my head. She had pinned a piece of paper onto the front of my shirt with a number and a letter on it. Grandma Boyer had visited the triangle house the night before to help my mom get me ready. She explained that the letter and number showed where my classroom would be so I didn't get lost.

"Your classroom will be 1K. And this label says Mike Stoneburner. Did you know you were named Mike after my brother? Be proud of your name," my Grandma Boyer said, as she tucked me into bed the night before my second first day of school.

Now most of the kids were walking through the entrance to the school. There were no cacti bowing along the way like soldiers. A breeze was drifting through much like the flow of children and some parents down the sidewalk.

The school was surrounded by trees and grassy fields. There was a playground out on the grass and a field with tall metal poles sticking out on either side of it. I recognised it as a football field from TV when my parents would watch the super bowl. I never saw a very large bowl of any food so it was boring. I stopped paying attention.

My mom nudged me again into the crowd and towards the badly painted white, bricked school. My stomach hurt and I tensed up. There was no line. People everywhere and I had no idea where to go except through the doors. There was no order. There was chaos. I reached for my mom's hand and clutched my stomach with the other. My guts felt like they were going to fall out so I held them back in. Then my mom's hand wasn't in mine. Instead, her hands gave me one last nudge and she rushed back to the car as horns from cars behind ours yelled at her.

She drove away.

I stared wide-eyed as the car space left by her filled with another. Another child hopped out of the car and rushed past me. I gulped and turned to the doors and followed the mass of children.

There was a hallway that led past a sign I could not decipher. Parents were standing there talking to a woman and shaking hands with a man in a suit. Following the other kids, I passed by a bigger area that led to a big dining hall where rows of tables sat empty waiting for lunch. I blindly followed everyone else. I found myself in a hallway that split off to different rooms. Above one of the doors I saw a letter and a number.

It was all like a puzzle and I understood, but I was still scared. I wasn't about to storm around like the rest of them. I had to be careful. I had to be safe. If only I were a superhero, they'd stand to one side. They'd be smiling at the new kid hero on his first day of school. They'd offer me toys and sandwiches, preferably peanut butter and jelly. I missed the twisted bowing cacti.

I couldn't stop walking or I'd get pushed and shoved, so I just followed any child who was as small as I was. I tried looking at their pinned papers to see what number and letter they had, but not every child had one. I grew more and more scared, so I took a deep breath. I imagined my mom had come in with me. She had kept holding my hand. Perhaps she even used her mom voice to make everyone stand aside. She'd holler a warrior's cry and hold up a sword and demand that we get through. Grandma Boyer would be waiting down the hallway pointing the way to my classroom so I could continue to learn to read more comics for my brother and Whiskey. I imagined my cat darting around the correct classroom, meowing at me to come in and jump up the curtains with her as she tore apart any student's work that was better than mine. I'd chase her away from their work and make new friends because I protected their things. Whiskey would swat at me from under the table playfully.

I groaned as my stomach reminded me that I was not my imagination. I looked around at the chaos again. I knew there were more people in Phoenix but it still seemed a lot here. I suddenly felt so small.

1K. My eyes saw the number first and then the letter. Right above the door in front of which stood a woman. I squealed out loud and clapped my hands. A few children passed by me giving me looks, but I darted through the people towards that magic number and that wonderful letter. I imagined my Grandma Boyer right behind me, too.

"Miss Young is your teacher," she had said the previous night and said now in my imagination. "She's new, so I don't know much about her. I was hoping you'd get Mrs. Eden, but she's not teaching Kindergarten this year. Mrs. Eden goes to our church. I have tea with her and the ladies every Wednesday. I've told her to look out for you."

Grandma Boyer's voice faded as I approached Miss Young, who stood at the classroom door.

I imagined my Grandma Boyer giving me a playful swat on my backside, "You be a good boy. Don't be a rotten little peanut. And you treat that lady nice."

Miss Young had curly brown hair like my mom and thick, plastic glasses like my grandma, but where my grandma had old, wrinkly skin, Miss Young had smooth pale skin; where my mom was short and stumpy, Miss Young was tall and chubby.

"1K?" she asked, looking down at my paper pinned to my shirt, "Yes. That's me."

Miss Young motioned me inside. I tried to get a good look at the classroom, but kids were everywhere. Some were crying. Some were singing; some were dancing and running. Some were picking their nose.

I took my finger out of my nose and thought it best to find my desk. After a minute, Miss Young came into the room, closed the door behind her, and called out to us in a sing-song voice that our names were on our desk. There was a great big surprise for all the students who found their names. I liked big surprises.

I imagined my Grandma Boyer taking me by the hand and leading me around the desks. "Your name is special. Don't let anyone tell you otherwise. You already know your letters, so let's get you ready to spell your name. Mike. It begins with an M, followed by an I, followed by a K, followed by an E."

I eventually found my desk and sat down.

Miss Young was at the front and with her song-like voice, she exclaimed, "Now everyone, in the morning after everyone is seated, we will stand up and begin with the Pledge of Allegiance."

Everyone stood up and I wondered why I even sat down in the first place.

"Now everyone, put your hand on your chest like this," she said, putting her right hand on her chest to show us. "And repeat after me…"

She looked around, nodding her head at each child until she stopped at me. "No, Michael, the other hand, please."

I looked at the other kids and saw that everyone else had their right hands on their chest.

"Use your right hand," I heard Miss Young say.

During that summer before starting school, Grandma Boyer had a family get together in the room along the garage where the long dining-room table fit the adults. A smaller table in the back fit the children. An elderly relative had come to kiss us all on the cheek and pretend to steal our noses. She asked us if we were enjoying our meal. I had been taught to treat old people nicely, so I smiled and answered her questions first.

"Oh, you poor dear," she sighed, looking down at my left hand as it scooped up pumpkin pie into my gob. She reached down and grabbed the fork and placed it into my right hand. "When I was teaching school, I used to tie the left hand behind the inflicted child's back so they learned to use the right hand."

I stared at the fork in my right hand as if the utensil had changed somehow. I didn't know how to hold it. The fork felt loose. I quickly changed it back, not understanding a word the old lady was saying.

My Grandma Boyer seemed to appear suddenly and shoo the old lady away. She knelt down next to me. "Don't pay any attention to her, Mike. You were born the way God made you. Just the way you are. Left-handed. You are all right, and don't let anyone tell you otherwise."

As I stood listening to Miss Young's instructions, I understood that the right hand was to be used. I knew most people were right-handed and that I was different.

I looked back at Miss Young and smiled. She walked over to me and wiggled each of her hands. "This is the right hand and this is the left."

I nodded, and she nodded back before moving back to the front. She looked up at the flag I recognised from the other school. It was the American flag. It waved in front of all the schools. Red and white stripes. Blue box with white stars. It represented the country I lived in.

"Now," Miss Young continued, "every morning we will stand behind our desk. Hand on our chest. Looking at the flag of the United States of America. It tells us where we live. We will say a pledge that promises our loyalty to our country. So, repeat after me …"

She began again and looked over at me. Her eyes darted down at my left hand resting on my chest. Her sweet smiled faltered and she came over to me again as she said, "I pledge allegiance…"

We all repeated the words after her, as she continued to slide closer to me. She kept facing the flag, but I could see her eyes come back to me.

"…to the flag…" she continued, and was soon right next to me, "…of the United States of America…"

She reached down and took my right hand and whispered, "This is our right hand."

"…and to the republic…" she sang out to us. We struggled with the word republic, but finally we got it while she showed me again which hand I should use.

She frowned again, her smooth skin wrinkling more. She walked back to the front and finished, "…for which it stands…one nation…under God…indivisible…with liberty and justice for all."

I imagined my Grandma Boyer standing next to me holding her left hand to her heart and saying the pledge with me.

"Left-handed people," I heard my Grandma Boyer say to me as I sat down after Miss Young told us to be seated. "We are a rare and an exotic breed of human. There is only a small percentage of us in this world, and you will understand when I say this: it is a right-handed world."

I was still scared, but I didn't want the teacher to know it. I didn't want the other students to know it, either. I wanted to show the teacher how clever I was. I needed her to see I could do things, so that she could tell my dad and mom that I hadn't given up on all the hopes and all the dreams. I needed my dad to be happy. I needed my mom to be safe. I needed the bath to be used to clean us, not to take out cactus needles and skunk spray.

The truth was though that I was terrified. What if I wasn't smart in this school? The teacher already thought I didn't know my left and my right. I had made her sad and I didn't know how to fix it. I wanted to talk to the other children and know their names. I wanted to know what they liked. I wanted to know if they loved superheroes and comics and cartoons. I wanted to know if they had an awesome cat like I did or one grandma that played the tambourine, and another whom cheated at board games.

As the school year went on, I'd find myself mostly going back to Grandma Boyer's house while my parents worked. We'd sit around her small end table in front of the couches and she'd set up her board games and we would play.

"Be the best that you can be." She smiled as she won another game of Sorry.

She had cheated again and I wasn't going to let her. "You have to move the right number, Grandma."

My grandma sat back with another grin. "I don't have to do anything I don't want to do."

"You're not following the rules," I said.

My grandma nodded, "But sometimes the rules aren't fair. What do you do then if things aren't fair?"

I shrugged.

"You ask questions. 'Why?' is a very important question," she explained, cleaning her glasses.

"Why are you cheating?" I asked quickly.

"Because I want to win," my grandma answered.

"Why?" I asked quickly again.

"I do follow the rules. It's just that I like driving you crazy more," she laughed, putting her glasses back on.

"You have rules. I follow your rules," I said.

"I am an adult," she winked, "I don't have to follow all the rules."

"That's not fair," I said.

"Adults don't always follow the rules. Better get used to it."

"That's not fair," I repeated. "It's mean."

"Adults can be mean."

"You're not mean. You love me."

"Fine," she giggled, "I'll follow the rules. Just for you. Because you're clever and learn quickly. Also, because I love you."

She moved her token back to where it was supposed to be. "Your turn, but I'll still win. So, how's school going? Learning to sit still yet?"

I shook my head.

"Concentrating on your work?"

I nodded.

"Being the best that you can be?"

I nodded again and sighed, "She likes to be a teacher. She's always helping me. She reminds me to sit still and pay attention. She tells me to sit up straight and to raise my hand before speaking. She says that a lot."

Grandma Boyer chuckled, "I bet she does."

That night, as I lay in bed and cuddled with Whiskey purring against my neck, I dreamt of the Alphabet People marching through the hallways of the Coleman school, led by Miss Young. The Alphabet People were the letters of the alphabet that were drawn to look like people. It was like having cartoons in the classroom. Each Alphabet person would have a sentence. Grandma Boyer told me they used alliteration because the same letter was used over and over again.

Miss Young kept barking orders at everyone. I didn't like it. I don't know why, but I didn't like being told what to do, especially if I already did it. When she snapped and got angry, it reminded me of my dad.

It was difficult to get used to staying in my desk all the time. At my first school, when I finished with my work, I got up and went to the floor and did activities and played. Here we were constantly moving in groups. We were almost like the flocks of geese that started to fly over Coleman's skies as they headed south. Miss Young explained they were heading to warmer weather when I asked her.

"Why can't I flock to the floor when I'm finished with my work?"

Miss Young frowned and my heart leapt into my throat. I didn't mean to make her frown when I asked questions.

"I know things were different at your other school, but this is my classroom and I do things differently."

I nodded and wanted to ask more questions, but Miss Young turned back to the class and continued walking around helping others trace their letters and write them in different sizes.

Then she came over to me and looked down at my paper. "You're finished already?"

"Yes, Miss Young," I said, lifting my head off my arm in hopes she'd give me something else to do.

"Well done, Michael," she said, patting my head.

I beamed up at her. "At my last school, we already visited the Alphabet People in the land of Alpha. I feel sorry that we visit them so much. They just want to be left alone, especially Mr. M. Can we write words now? I can write words like Mike, magic, Michael Jackson, motorcycle and Mighty Mouse. All the important words."

Miss Young stamped her foot and I nearly jumped out of my chair. She had scared me.

"Michael," she hissed, "you are disturbing the rest of the class and need to behave."

I blinked up at her. I didn't know what I had done wrong.

Miss Young was looking at me sadly, "I know you already had a year of school in your fancy city, but you're in Coleman now. Not everyone has practised their letters. I need to teach them and you need to sit quietly and wait."

Things were much slower as the weeks passed and summer faded into fall. Instead of the tasks changing from day to day like I got used to in Phoenix, I found myself repeating tasks over and over for a week. Some days I was so tired of it I'd sigh. The other kids would notice. Miss Young would frown and sometimes she'd stomp her foot and tell me to keep my comments to myself.

So, I'd imagine the alphabet and numbers had come alive and could talk to me as I drew them into my writing notebook. It was a gray-paged booklet with blue lines. I'd sing their songs to them that the teacher had taught me in Phoenix. I'd draw their letters around the page pretending they were moving around.

I was in the middle of one of the battles. The Twos were shooting at Ms. W, who was being protected by Ms. A and her awesome sneeze and Mr. R, who would tie the twos up with his ribbons. A shadow formed above my desk. I slowly looked up to see Miss Young.

"What have you done to your paper?" she said.

I looked down at it. The war was ugly. There were many Twos tied up and many Alphabet People hurt. I looked back up at her.

"Michael, your imagination gets you into trouble," she growled, "and you have made a mess of your work. You'll have to do it again."

She grabbed my paper and tore it up and threw it in the bin. My mouth dropped open as I imagined W, A, and R screaming because of the sudden earthquake that tore up their world. Not to mention I wanted to scream because I didn't want to do it again.

She turned away from me and clapped her praying hands together. "Anyone else scribbling all over their pages will get their work ripped up and thrown out, too. You'll have to start all over just like Michael."

Everyone looked at me and I got red and hot in the face, and I looked down at my hands. I didn't think my page was messy. I was just writing the letters over and over. I was just having fun while I waited till everyone else was ready to do our next work.

Later in the school year, Miss Young moved me. She told to sit at a desk right in front of hers. I froze, wondering if this was a good or a bad thing. "Don't worry, Michael. It's so I can see what fantastic work you do."

I grinned and ran to my desk now closer to hers. She seemed surprised that I was happy with her decision.

One day, Miss Young introduced us to the letter M. It was written up on the chalk board next to a printed out coloured picture of Mr. M. He was my favourite letter of them all. We had a lot in common.

At my desk I called over to Miss Young and said, "We are doing the letter M today. It's my favourite."

"Yes. Today we are going to Mmmmmeet, Mmmmmister, EMmmmmmmmmm! A lot of things start with Mr. M, like Mmmmilk, Mmmmmouse, but --"

"First," she sighed, looking down at me and then the whole class, "it's time for our Pledge of Allegiance. It's the first duty of the day. Right hands on your heart please. Stand behind your chairs. Eyes on the flag. Everyone ready?"

I had my right hand on my chest, but it felt wrong. It didn't feel like me. Just like the way she wanted me to hold my pencil. But she said all of those things were wrong. Which meant, how I felt, how I wanted to be, was wrong, wasn't it? I didn't know. Thinking about it made me sad. So instead, I imagined my Grandma Boyer stepping up next to me with her left hand on her heart, "Don't worry. I'm an adult. I don't have to follow the rules."

She winked at me and I giggled. I couldn't wait till I was an adult. I'd put my left hand on my heart. I'd hold my pencil the way I wanted and I wouldn't be angry or violent.

We said the pledge and sat down. Miss Young came over to me and said, "Thank you for reciting the pledge properly, Michael. Don't think I didn't notice. Good boy."

I grinned. It was difficult making Miss Young happy. I had been trying for most of the year.

"Now, Mr. M has a Mighty, Munching Mouth! He can say Marvellous and Meaningful words and likes to eat Mouth-watering Melons!"

I sat on the edge of my seat. I liked this guy. He was nice. We had a lot in common, and I liked to use marvellous and meaningful words. True, I didn't know many yet, but I still liked to listen to them. I also loved eating all sorts of melons! Mr. M and Mike, that's me, were the best of friends. Our pages were handed out and we began writing. I was closer to the window now. The leaves from the trees in the distance were finishing falling off into the browning grass. I knew Mr. M well, and quickly traced his letter. I wrote his letter out as I did many times with my name. In a matter of moments, I was finished.

A shadow appeared above my desk. I looked up slowly and smiled.

"Michael," Miss Young said, wrinkles around her lips and eyes. "You're holding your pencil incorrectly again. We've talked about this." She reached towards my left hand. "That left hand is really causing you problems, isn't it?"

I let her take the pencil from me and she held it in her right hand. "You see, you hold the pencil like this. Right on your ring finger, but that's wrong. You need to hold it like this. Just near the tip, you rest it on your middle finger. Middle finger. Like this. Keep your back straight when sitting. Your head needs to be straight. I've told you this. Correct posture means correct penmanship."

I liked writing but I didn't like penmanship.

"Try it, Michael," Miss Young said, handing me back my pencil. I copied the way she held it. My left hand didn't feel as if it had a strong grip on it. I sat up straight and kept my head straight too.

"Now, write some Ms for me, Michael," she smiled.

I looked down at the paper but I had a problem. My left hand was blocking the tip of my pencil. I couldn't see where I was writing.

I tried writing a few Ms, but as I moved my left hand across to the right it smeared the scribbled Ms I had managed to complete. My page looked like it did with the war between the Twos and R, A and W.

My pencil slipped from my hand and I held it my way. My wrist bent and my head tilted. I wrote magnificent letter Ms.

"No, Michael," Miss Young snapped and pulled the pencil from my hand and showed me again. "You're making your page messy."

I looked down at my page. The only mess on there was from doing it her way.

Miss Young's eyes widened, "Mr. M does not love messy work. He loves making marvellous work."

I nodded, taking the pencil from her and writing my way. The letters looked like the dotted lined ones. They weren't wobbly. They almost looked exactly the same.

"Michael, you need to hold your pencil correctly."

"But it's messy," I whispered.

I didn't understand. Miss Young's way created a mess, but she didn't want a mess. My way made marvellous work. Sure, my feet tapped when I wrote. My wrist was bent. My hand was twisted. My pencil rested on my ring finger, held by my middle finger and steered with my thumb. But to her it was an abnormal way I had to come up with to write well in a right-handed world.

I could hold the pencil the way she wanted me to, but I wasn't able to write as neatly as I would have liked. I wasn't able to feel comfortable writing, and I wasn't able to avoid smearing the pencil lead with my hand and keeping my back straight. So, I chose what was best for me. I held the pencil my way in order to get the job done.

Miss Young did not see it that way and I couldn't really explain it well. She stomped her foot and pointed at my paper and scolded, "Michael Stoneburner!"

I winced. My mom said my name like that when I was in serious trouble.

"If it is one thing I will not tolerate in my classroom is a child who will not hold their pencil correctly! Now, I showed you twice. You know how to do it. So do it!"

She knelt down beside me and held her pen how she wanted me to hold it. Middle finger.

I imagined Grandma Boyer clicking her tongue at Miss Young, "Such a rude finger. Why would anyone want to use such a rude finger? Ring fingers are nicer and hold pretty things when we get older."

I held up my middle finger at her. "My grandma doesn't like me using this finger. I want to put it on this one. You wear pretty rings on this one. I want to, too, one day."

She gasped and pushed my hand down. "Michael, you need to hold your pencil the way I have shown you."

"No," I said, "I don't like it."

I don't know what was wrong with me, but I knew saying no to her was wrong. I knew raising my voice at her was wrong. I knew arguing with a teacher would get me into trouble, but I was feeling a tightness in my chest. My heart wouldn't leave my throat. My ears were ringing. My skin felt like it was starting to catch fire.

"Tough, young man, you must write this way in MY CLASSROOM!" she roared and stomped her foot multiple times and slammed her hands onto my desk. I jumped up and stepped back. My body was trembling. Her shadow loomed over my desk. She continued to stomp her feet. Her hands slammed down again and again onto my desk as she screamed down at me. My imagination turned Miss Young into my dad. I slid out of my desk.

I could hear Miss Young scream at me but I could only see my dad saying it, "What are you doing, young man? Get back into your seat!"

My mouth hung open as I imagined cacti behind me. I imagined the desks flying around. I imagined Miss Young hurting me.

I screamed. And pushed my desk at her and ran. The desk tipped over and she cried out, but I kept running straight out of the classroom.

Mr. Molly's Cutting Board

Throughout the year I started getting sent to the principal's office almost daily. Miss Young wouldn't even try to correct me anymore. When I would automatically put my left hand over my heart for the pledge, she'd send me to the office. When she caught me holding my pencil incorrectly, she'd send me to the office. If I called out too many times, she'd send me to the office. It might as well have been my new classroom.

Mr. Molly's office smelt like onions and dust. He had a big handled board hanging from his wall that looked like what my Grandma Boyer used to cut up vegetables and meats. His office had an old wooden table with chairs. Papers were piled up in one corner of his desk. He had a notepad in another and a phone in the other corner with its cord dangling off to the side. He was always on the phone when I came in. His grey hair made his black hair sparkle. His glasses were on the tip of his nose much like my grandma had hers when she was focusing. He would be scribbling something down on his notepad. His throat vibrated with noises that sounded like he was agreeing with the person he was talking to on the phone.

Mr. Molly would instruct me to sit down on a chair across from his desk. My legs dangled over the chair in the corner. My legs were too small to reach the floor but I wasn't small enough to get me up into the chair. Sometimes he'd help me up onto the chair by yanking my arm up quickly and swinging me into it. I preferred to help myself after that. He'd sit in his seat and I'd sit there in silence while he wrote things down or talked on the phone. Sometimes he'd take me back to class and found a teary Miss Young struggling to teach the rest of our class.

"No," she sometimes said, "I don't want him back in here."

And on the day I ran out and tipped over my desk, she added, "He threw a desk at me. He refused to listen to instructions and threw his desk. He has terrified the other students. He is a huge disruption, and I can't handle him anymore. Call his parents. Send him home."

The principal looked down at me with wild eyes. They reminded me of my father's eyes when he was angry and drinking. I was terrified of Mr. Molly. He looked back up at her. "Are you all right? Did the desk hit you?"

Miss Young wiped a few tears from her cheeks, "I'll be okay. The desk was heavy, but I'm sure I'll be fine."

The principal was holding my hand. I was startled to hear him speak to me. "Young man, you're coming with me. We are calling home. We do not throw desks at teachers here in this school nor do we disrupt the class and refuse to follow instructions."

I was trembling with fear and confusion. I didn't remember scaring the other students. Looking at them now, they were busy doing their work. None of them seemed to care what I was doing. I looked at my desk that was still overturned. I didn't remember throwing the desk, but I remembered how I felt. I had been terrified and angry. Maybe I did do that?

I wiped my own tears away. I wanted to hug Miss Young and say sorry, but the principal had too strong of a grip on my hand. It almost hurt. I closed my eyes and then opened them in horror. What if I was like The Incredible Hulk? What if when I got angry I turned into a big monstrous beast that could lift his desk above his head and throw it at his teachers?

"I'm sorry," I blurted out to Miss Young, "I didn't mean to throw my desk at you."

The principal jerked me away from the classroom door.

He pulled me back to his office and lifted me up by my arm and put me in the chair across his desk and reach for the phone to call my parents. There was no answer so he dialed on the phone again.

Before he made the call, he scolded me. "Young man, your actions have caused a huge disruption to this school. I want you to think about that. Think about your actions. You got angry and hurt your teacher. You scared your fellow classmates, and now I've had to stop my busy schedule to try and call your parents, who aren't home and don't have time to deal with your problems. I now have to call your emergency contact."

I gulped. I caused an emergency? How hurt was Miss Young? She was limping. I looked down at my legs and feet. I couldn't remember getting so angry and frustrated like this before. I never hurt someone before. I didn't like it. I got angry and I hurt someone.

I began to cry.

The principal then spoke on the phone, over my tears. "I trust Miss Young. If she says he threw a desk at her then I believe her."

I cried harder.

"I have counselled Miss Young on numerous occasions on behaviour management with your grandson."

I was just like my dad, wasn't I? When I got angry, I hurt people.

"Miss Young would not have warranted having a desk being toppled onto her legs," he stammered into the phone.

I looked up at him and wiped away my tears. I didn't want to be a monster. I didn't like feeling angry or frustrated. I wasn't going to get angry again. I wasn't going to hurt anyone ever again.

"Yes," he urged into the phone, "I expect you to believe Michael has refused to follow instructions and has disrupted the class by throwing a desk at Miss Young."

He listened. His free hand was tapping a pencil against his desk. "No, but Mrs. Boyer, I can assure you --"

He tried to continue speaking, but I could now hear Grandma Boyer's voice murmur from the phone. He held the receiver slightly away from his ear. His face was getting red. A vein was appearing on his forehead.

"I expect you to come get him," he said, but she must have said no because he continued, "What do you mean you refuse? Of course I will correct this situation, but..."

He listened again, "Yes, ma'am."

He went back to making the noises that vibrated his throat before he hung up the phone and sighed, "She's a feisty one."

I nodded.

He stood up and looked over at his cutting board hanging from the wall, "Well, young man, no one will be picking you up, however, I cannot let you return to class without you learning your lesson. You cannot disrupt your class. You cannot ignore your teacher's instructions, and despite your grandmother disbelieving you have thrown a desk at your teacher, I cannot let that go unpunished as well."

I nodded again.

He stood up and pulled his cutting board off of the wall and returned to his desk and sat down. "Come here, Michael."

I slipped off the chair and walked around the desk to him.

He had wild eyes again. "You will not do this again. Face my desk please. Hands on the desk."

My eyes widened. Was he going to use the cutting board to chop my fingers off? I began to tremble.

"This will not happen again!" he snapped and pulled his chair back away from his desk and stood, holding the board.

I turned my head to look at him.

"Face forward!" he barked, and I looked towards the door leading out to where the office lady was doing her work. Suddenly there was a loud wack and pain shot across my backside. I sobbed loudly, but the door stayed closed. There was one more wack and another sting.

The principal hung the board back on the wall and told me to straighten up.

"I will take you back to class," he said "but if you are sent back here again today. I will paddle you again."

Not all cutting boards were used to cut food. I learnt that some of them were used to punish. When I was back in class, I didn't say a word as I sat down in pain. I held my pencil the way Miss Young wanted and said sorry when she scolded me for messy work, even though Mr. M

110

didn't seem to mind. For the first time ever, I wished I was right-handed.

I didn't tell anyone. I just accepted the punishment. It is what happened when someone was naughty. The Willow Tree. My mom swatted me sometimes. My dad's wild eyes and terrible temper. And now, Mr. Molly's Cutting Board. I wasn't a stranger to getting a good paddling. So, I didn't think anything was wrong with what the principal did. Besides, there were many other students who got hit at school. I saw them come out of the principal's office with the same limp as I did.

The Plastic Blob

Miss Young gave the class a present. It was a soft plastic object. I thought it was a bouncy ball and tried to bounce it on my desk. It did bounce, but Miss Young scolded me and told me it wasn't a toy. It was a pencil holder. She showed us how to slip it onto our pencils. She showed us how our fingers rested in each groove.

I crinkled my nose and looked down at this torture device, this blob of soft plastic, that had grooves where your middle finger rested, the pointer finger rested, and the thumb. It was terrible, and I already hated it. Miss Young would not let me write unless I had one of those holders on my pencil with my fingers resting in place. She would stand at my desk during handwriting and constantly put it back on. It got to the point where she would just grab my hand and squeezed it until my fingers were crushed against the soft plastic of the pencil holder.

Towards the end of the year, Miss Young finally had enough of me. I was still struggling with listening to her during handwriting. I just couldn't do it her way. She broke down crying. Out of her nose like molten lava, dripped the gooiest, slimiest snot I had ever seen in my five-year-old life.

The snot flowed over her lips as she sobbed at me, "You have to hold the pencil correctly. You have to do your work. You have to stay quiet. Teaching shouldn't be this hard. Why did my first year in the classroom have to be with you?"

She howled and slammed her hand on my desk, scaring the life out of me. She grabbed my hand again and squeezed harder. It brought tears to my eyes.

She kicked at my desk and stormed away from me frantically getting back to her own desk.

I threw the pencil at Miss Young.

I wish I had powers like the mutants did in the X-Men comics my dad read. One mutant could lift her hands and move things with her mind. She was known as the Phoenix, and she was my favourite. I would have done the same thing with the pencil. I would have called it back to me. I lifted my hands to my face.

The flying pencil did somersaults in the air. I could see it. Like slow motion. It squealed with glee as it landed directly into the back of her hair and stuck there, eraser showing.

She had hurt me, and I wanted her to go away and leave me alone. She was like a villain in the comic books. She hurt people.

Miss Young pulled the pencil out of the back of her hair, turned around, face full of mucus, and screamed the loudest scream I'd ever heard. She ran out of the room like a maniac. I didn't even look at the other students. I couldn't hear anything except the beating of my heart. My hand was still throbbing from where she squeezed it against that terrible plastic blob.

After I calmed down, I started to hear that some students were crying. I looked over at them. They just looked between the doorway where the teacher had left and me. I wondered if Miss Young was calling my mom and dad. Maybe she thought it was her turn to get a paddling from the principal because she had hurt me and ruined my work again.

Mr. Molly took me out of class and I didn't see Miss Young again until school was over and my mom and dad showed up. I was sitting in Mr. Molly's office. He had paddled me again so I was trying to sit in the chair across his desk without hurting so much. My parents both had those wild eyes that I hate. My dad had never come to this school before. They came inside Mr. Molly's office and stood near me. No one spoke to me. We waited till Mr. Molly returned with Miss Young following.

As soon as she saw my parents, Miss Young burst into tears again. "Your son. Your son. This is my first year of teaching and Michael makes me want to quit. He isn't ready for school. He isn't prepared. He needs to repeat this class again. He's too young. He isn't like the other children. He needs time to grow up."

114

Getting In The Way

In Phoenix, I was ready for school but Miss Young said I wasn't. She said that I wasn't like the other children. I was different. I needed to grow up. My parents were angry. The grown-ups shouted at each other. Mr. Molly ended up getting me to sit outside with the office lady.

I didn't understand why I did things differently that made others uncomfortable or upset. I didn't want Miss Young to cry with snot bubbles. I didn't want to do my work messy. I didn't want to hold my pencil incorrectly. Was my dad right? Was I a curse?

I ended the school year with Mr. Molly and Miss Young trying to tell my parents that I had to repeat Kindergarten again. It would be my third time. They refused to do so and signed a paper from the school to allow me to go into the first grade.

"Grandma," I said over my plate of pancakes, "I don't want to be left handed anymore."

Grandma put her fork down slowly and pushed her glasses back up her nose. She looked me over and folded her hands, "Why?"

"It gets me in trouble."

"Michael," she said in a soft voice that made me look her in the eyes, "you were born this way. God made you this way. Just because someone else doesn't like something about you, doesn't mean you stop that part of you. There are not that many left handed people in this world. You're so unique."

"But I'm first born," I said, "that makes me cursed."

My grandma's eyes widened and I was scared they were going to turn wild. I was scared she was finally going to see the truth about me.

"You are not cursed," she snapped, "Don't be ridiculous. You are a blessing. My special grandson. Now enough of this. Eat your pancakes."

With school over and my parents working, I still spent most of my days with Grandma Boyer. I was happy to get out of the A-frame, with its triangle shape and angled walls. I felt trapped in that house, and the summer in Michigan was beautiful. I loved the colour the world seemed to be now that I was far away from the desert. The dark greens of the leaves and grass soothed my eyes. I could smell each of the different flowers. The world was full of blues and purples, pinks and reds. I spent the summer exploring the woods surrounding our place when I wasn't at my grandma's house. And even when I was at her house, I explored the yard around her place. I explored through the trees and out back in her fields and ditches.

"You're all a bunch of little rascals," Grandma Boyer laughed as she stood there holding Christopher.

I was sitting in a little red wagon. My mom and my aunt were standing next to me. We were dressed up like a show they liked called the Little Rascals. I had on underwear and overalls.

"You all look fantastic," Grandma had said again. She was saying that a lot. "And you," she added, looking at me, "will steal the show. You're adorable." She was saying that a lot, too.

I loved being the centre of attention and Grandma Boyer loved to put me there. We were going to a thing called a parade where people dressed up, dressed their vehicles up and walked down the streets while others watched and cheered. We had a bucket full of candy we threw out to the crowd. Grandma Boyer was watching me carefully to make sure I didn't sneak any, but she kept missing the times my mom and my aunt stole one. I tried to tell Grandma Boyer on them but my mom and aunt shrieked and called me a traitor. We laughed. I wasn't sure why we were doing a parade accept that we were celebrating the town and we were representing the church that the Boyer family went to, but I wasn't too sure. It didn't matter because it was fun and it had candy.

The school holidays were fun when I was with Grandma Boyer. We played her board games. We talked and laughed. We sang songs. When my mom was home and not working, we'd all play together. My brother was growing older and babbled more. I made him laugh and helped feed him food from jars. Sometimes I would sneak a few bites of the banana custard baby food.

My mom caught me once, and only laughed. "When I was pregnant with you, I craved bananas, you little monkey. Leave your brother some."

I tried.

My brother and I would spend Saturday mornings watching cartoons. Dad would be quietly drinking his coffee in the kitchen on his days off. When he was working, he was on shift work, which meant he worked through the night and slept through the day. We weren't allowed to be in the same room as him when he woke up. We used to, but after the house burnt down, he had gone quiet. He rarely laughed.

I helped my mom clear off Christopher's highchair tray. We heard the fan from upstairs turn off. That meant my dad was waking up and we had to get out of the kitchen.

My mom grabbed my brother and took him into the living room. There was a larger crib on the floor that I sometimes pretended was a cage and Christopher was an animal in a zoo. He'd make animal noises when I named them. Sometimes he got them wrong and I'd correct them.

"Mike, hurry up and clear that off for me, okay?" my mom whispered before she disappeared into the other room.

I stood on my tiptoes and placed the empty jar and spoon on the counter near the sink. I saw Christopher's bib on the table and grabbed it. It had banana custard all over it. It needed washing and I stood there in panic. The laundry basket was upstairs. We didn't have a washing machine or dryer. We would have to travel into Coleman to the Laundromat where everyone else washed their clothes by putting quarters into the machines. My parents waited till we had all the clothes dirty before we did a big wash. I didn't know what to do with the bib. Mom told me to wash up but I couldn't take the bib upstairs so I couldn't decide whether to put it up on the counter or leave it on the table. I heard the stairs creak from the living room and knew my dad was coming. My heart leapt into my throat. I decided to put it back on the table and darted into the living room.

As I rounded the wall that separated the kitchen from the living room, a shadow crept in front of me and I slammed into it and went tumbling into the floor. I was too late. My father was downstairs and I had gotten in his way.

"Dean!" I heard my mom gasp, as the skin of my arm burnt against the carpet as I slid into the sliding glass door that led out to our front yard.

I couldn't help but cry instantly as my head slammed into the glass and my arm felt like it was on fire.

I heard the flick of his cigarette lighter as he lit up a cigarette inside the kitchen. My mom ran out to him as I picked myself up and made my way quietly to my brother, who was peering at me through his crib.

"What?" my dad muttered, "I haven't even had my coffee yet. I'm just waking up."

"He was trying to get out of your way," she sighed.

118

"I can't deal with this right now," he growled, "Can you get the coffee ready?"

I heard her do things in the kitchen and just stood there quietly looking at my brother. I couldn't wait to go to Grandma Boyer's house, but my dad had the night off. Mornings were better at Grandma Boyer's house. We could be as loud as we wanted. Most times, she'd be the one in the early hours pulling us out of bed with her songs.

Thundercats, HO!

"The bright sun comes up," Grandma Boyer sang softly from the bedroom door. I had spent the night like I usually did when dad worked a few nights in a row. I was already starting to smile. I pulled the blankets over my head trying to hide my giggles.

"The dew goes away," she continued to sing. Her voice was closer to the bed.

Giggles escaped my mouth and my body tensed up. I knew what was coming and it was terrifying and exciting.

"GOOD MORNING! GOOD MORNING!" she sang loudly, tickling me through the blankets. "The little birds say!"

That never happened with Dad. Things were quiet, except for the TV. And that's where I disappeared. Heroes lived in the television. My friends lived there. That's where I wanted to be when I was at home, forced into silence when dad woke up. His shadow loomed in the kitchen as he smoked his cigarettes and drank his coffee. But not here at Grandma Boyer's. It always smelled like summer inside her house. Warm. Sweet. Citrus.

I hated the smell of my dad's cigarettes, but when I complained, he'd blow smoke in my face over and over again. It was as if I were in the burning house again. I felt like I was suffocating. In the house with him. In the car with him. When I was around him, I just wanted to get away. I wanted space. Wide and open. Free from his cruelty. He wasn't a two-faced villain anymore. He was just a villain. When I was with Grandma Boyer, the villain couldn't get to me.

Just like the comics, TV cartoons taught me that heroes defeated villains. My dad could never stand up to Grandma Boyer. She turned him quiet. He watched his steps around her. He was miserable. He looked exactly how I felt when I was in the A-Frame. Still my favourite cartoon on TV, Thundercats taught me that I would be a hero if I were just like the young cub turned Lord, Lion-O. If I were more like him, I'd be able to defeat the villains like he did with the Mutants and Mummra the Ever Living each week. He'd have his friends, of

121

course, Cheetara, Tigra, Panthro and twin cubs. He'd also have his faithful pet, Snarf.

Grandma always reminded me that I was a boy whenever I went to the shops with her and we passed through the toy section. She'd also tell me which toys were for girls as well. I was walking through the toy section with my Grandma. My brother was nestled in her arms. Suddenly my eyes fell upon a line of toys hanging from a metal hook. My eyes lit up at the red circle with a black image of a feline with its mouth open. The word "Thundercats" in silver brown and yellow etched across the top of the packaging and in gold was the name "Lion-O". I squealed. Underneath clear packaging was a Lion-O toy with his red, wavy mane.

"Michael," Grandma Boyer hissed, "control yourself. We're in public."

I stopped bouncing around pointing at the toy, "It's Lion-O. And there's Tigra. Cheetara. Panthro. Oh, Grandma Boyer, look, there's even Mumm-Ra!"

She knew I liked this cartoon. I would watch it when it was on at her house.

"Boys and their toys," Grandma sighed, shaking her head, "My sons always loved their small, green army men. We'd buy buckets of them. They never took care of them, though. I always found them around the house and in the yard with the bottom of my feet."

I reached up towards the Cheetara figurine and my Grandma playfully slapped at my hand and hissed, "Don't touch. Just look. Besides, that's a female toy and it's for the girls. The others are for the boys."

"But I like Cheetara," I smiled, "She's my favourite. Oh I wish we could buy them all."

"$5.99 for a toy?" My Grandma shook her head, "Those are expensive. Come on. Let's go."

We left the store and suddenly I realized I had new hopes and dreams. I wanted those toys so badly. If I had them, I could have my own adventures. I could take them with me and I wouldn't leave them

around like my uncles had done when they were kids with their toys.
I'd protect them, especially from fires.

On my next birthday, I woke up to the smell of pancakes and laughter.
My mom, Christopher and I stayed over at my Grandma Boyer's
house. My dad had to work the night before and after work he'd stop
by and we'd all go home after I opened my presents. I slipped out of
my bed and walked out to the kitchen. My mom and Grandma were
finishing off making breakfast. Both of them had aprons on that they
wore when they cooked. I was already excited and tried to run out to
the living room where I had found my presents wrapped up on the
coffee table in front of the couches.

"Oh no you don't," Grandma Boyer quickly said, "Breakfast first. We
wait for your father and then presents and cake."

I slowly turned around with a mischievous smile. "Naww, I want to
open them."

Christopher was sitting off to the side of the kitchen in a highchair
babbling and playing with a large wooden spoon. When he saw me, he
grinned and waved his hand with the spoon in it. He didn't have a
strong enough grip and it flung towards me and clattered on the floor.
My eyes widened but I still laughed and picked it up.

"I wish Whiskey could have been here," I said.

My mom shook her head, "It'd be silly to keep having her come all the
way here and back again. She likes the outdoors. The woods are
perfect for her to have fun."

We finished breakfast and for a few moments we waited in the living
room talking to each other as my Grandma Boyer and mom crocheted
together. They made the most beautiful doilies that could decorate

tables and chairs. They had threads of all different colours. They didn't stop until Grandma's phone rang on the wall near the kitchen.

She got up and answered, "Hello? Oh, are you still at work? At home?! Why in heavens are you there? Oh. Yes. Yes, you may."

My mom had been listening to that conversation and was already up near Grandma Boyer when she handed the phone over and snapped, "It's your husband. He isn't coming."

My mom grabbed the phone and took it down the hall out of sight until the cord of the phone became tight. When she came back, she just hung up the phone and clapped her hands, "Well, let's open these presents and get on the road."

I watched Grandma Boyer's lips tighten but she didn't say a word. She just put a present into my lap and finally broke into a smile, "You can have your own tribe now."

I had the sick feeling in my stomach that suddenly went away when I opened the first present and saw Lion-O's figurine. I squealed. The second present had Panthro. The third one had Mumm-Ra. I hugged them to my body grinning from ear to ear.

"I love turning 6!" I exclaimed. "Thank you, Grandma! Thank you, Mom!"

"You were born in Phoenix, Mike," Grandma Boyer said to me one afternoon on a weekend I stayed at her place.

I had showed her a comic I was reading. It was a sad comic. One of my heroes had died and she wanted to know why I was crying. I pointed to a red-headed woman with a green and gold outfit and a flaming bird on the costume of her chest.

"This is Jean Gray. She's my favourite. She's called The Phoenix. What does this say?"

Grandma Boyer peered through her glasses on the tip of her nose and read, "I am fire incarnate!"

"What's that mean?"

"It means she is made of living fire. What is she?"

I nodded, "She's a superhero in the X-Men, but she died."

"Did you know there is a creature called a phoenix, too?"

"Like her?

My grandma shook her head and rolled her eyes, "You should be liking G.I. Joe and He-Man. But, anyway, no, not superheroes. There is a bird called a phoenix. It is a great and powerful bird that no matter what happens to it, no matter how bad life gets for it, it is reborn."

"Reborn?"

"When the phoenix dies, it bursts into flames and all that's left is a pile of ash, but in that ash, there is an egg and out of this egg the phoenix is reborn. It survives and is even more powerful than before."

"Just like the superhero!" I exclaimed.

Grandma sighed, let go of me, and walked over to her bookshelf and pulled a book off the shelf. She sat back down next to me and flipped through a few pages.

"Mike," she said, pointing to a picture of a beautiful bird with wings of flames, "you are strong. Just like me. Stubborn, too, but I'll deny I ever said I was. No matter what happens to you, always love. No matter what happens, always laugh. Things will happen in your life that may hurt you, or there may be terrible events, but you have my blood in you. You will rise up and be better for it. You are my little phoenix."

She kissed my forehead and put her arms around me again. I stared quietly at the picture as she read aloud the myth of the phoenix. I loved it already. She even flipped through to other pages and taught me about the unicorn and the fairies and the ogres and trolls. I listened and hugged my grandma tighter.

"I'm happy I have you," I whispered to her.

"I'm happy I have you, too," she whispered back, and we spent the afternoon reading about magical creatures. My imagination loved it, and I thought up wonderful stories where I was riding a unicorn with a phoenix on my shoulder. We travelled through a mythical land, destroying ogres and trolls.

The Shadow Monster

I don't know why, but my dad's eyes started to become surrounded by dark circles. He stopped shaving until the shadow spread across his face and grew into a beard. It became even more important to stay silent in the morning. He smoked more. He drank more. On his days off, we no longer left the house. We'd only leave if we were staying at Grandma Boyer's house. We learnt to only talk to him after he talked to us. Even then, if he felt ignored, he'd get angry. Our house felt like the floors were thin ice. We had to be careful where we walked or cracks would appear in his smile. He could be happy one moment and then suddenly terrifying if we seemed to blink wrong.

My dad had woken the night before. He wasn't happy about going into work. He was smoking and pacing about a manager that he didn't like. The manager was always telling him how to do his job and nothing he did seemed to be good enough.

"Does he know Miss Young?" I asked, because he sounded a lot like my Kindergarten teacher.

"Don't be stupid," my dad snapped, "and mind your own business! I can't even talk in this house without someone listening!"

I should have known better than to try and talk to him when he first woke up. I couldn't help but hear him. He was pacing from the kitchen into the living room. He was speaking so loudly.

My mom tried to sooth him back in the kitchen but he only got louder, "Why can't I just wake up in peace? Why do they always have to be around?"

I winced at his words and lost myself in playing silently with my toys. I had Lion-O defeat Mumm-Ra. Christopher was asleep in the caged-crib next to me in the living room. He was lucky he could sleep through anything.

After awhile my mom, her eyes damp from crying, came into the living room and scooped up Christopher, startling him out of a snore, "Michael, pack up your toys. You're going to grandma's house."

"Mom, are you okay?" I asked while I did what I was told.

127

She tried to speak but it almost broke into a sob so she stopped herself and only nodded. She went into the kitchen with Christopher in her arms. I heard my dad mutter something but I was too busy feeling sick to my stomach. I was terrified. I didn't want to walk into the kitchen. I wanted to stay in the living room with the toys in my arms. I looked down at Lion-O. I thought about what he would do. He would hold his sword up to his eyes and try to see if there was danger.

So I held up the sword to my face and closed my eyes. I repeated what Lion-O would say in the cartoon, "Sword of Omens, give me sight beyond sight."

I imagined my dad in the kitchen. A shadow over his face. I guess working nights makes that happen to people. I'd have to avoid looking at him. If I looked at him, he'd get angry. I wasn't sure why but he didn't like being looked at when he first woke up. He didn't like anyone in his space, either, so I'd have to walk quickly through the kitchen. I'd have to run.

So I did. I put the Sword of Omens down and I bolted through the living room and into the kitchen. I tried darting passed him as he sat at the table smoking his cigarette and drinking his coffee. I paid more attention to where he was at than my balance and I toppled over and fell. He didn't scoop me up. He didn't check to make sure I was okay. He just got loud and angry and that's when I made sure to never run in the house again.

We spent a lot of time at Grandma Boyer's house when dad needed his own space. I wanted to just live there again. I wanted to wake up and have pancakes everyday. People who ate pancakes were always smiling. One day after picking us up after work, my mom was quiet when she got to Grandma's house, so much so my grandma knew something was wrong, too. We both hovered near her as she tried to pretend everything was okay. She just talked about work and talked to Christopher about the mess of food all over his face.

My grandma pulled her aside and they spoke quietly. They always spoke quietly when they were talking about my dad. I tried to listen as best as I could. I'd hear them say "he" a lot and "Dean" and "I love him." and "He's just sick right now."

"Call me!" Grandma Boyer called out when we drove away.

The car ride was in silence. Mom did not play the radio. We didn't sing. We didn't play any car games. I tried, but she didn't respond. Her hands were white against the steering-wheel. She didn't speak until we pulled onto Barden Road that led to our house. It was as if the moment we went from pavement to dirt and stone broke something inside of her. The sun had set. Usually when we got home, we'd watch TV, or I'd help her put Christopher to bed. She had other plans this evening.

I tried asking her, "How long is dad going to be sick?"

"When we get home, you go straight to bed," she said quickly, ignoring my question.

I started talking to her about random things, like unicorns and phoenixes and Thundercats, but she ignored all that.

"I mean it, Michael. Do you understand? Straight to bed."

"Am I in trouble?"

She didn't answer.

"I'm sorry," I whispered, not sure why I was apologising, but I wanted to fix it. My stomach was starting to hurt.

"What?" she said, her eyes blinking rapidly, "Oh no. No, no. You're not in trouble. You just need to go to bed. Dad needs silence."

I immediately stopped talking. I thought about the last time I didn't give my dad his morning silence he brought out his belt and snapped it in front of me. The air and sound scared me into tears.

"Okay," I said quietly, and noticed my brother's babbling even stopped.

When we pulled into our driveway that looped around the house, I saw there were no lights on. I wondered if he was even home or if he was already in bed. Maybe that's why I had to be quiet. I got out of the car and stood at the back porch.

"Whiskey!" I called out. She loved to explore the woods around the house, but she knew at night to be nearby when I called. She'd always come running. I'd hear her meow before I saw her. I think she lived out in the woods whenever I was away and she didn't come with us.

My mom rushed over to me and covered my mouth. "Michael, go in the house. Get straight to bed."

"But Whiskey," I started, but she stopped me.

"Not tonight," she hissed. "Go." Mom hurried back to the car to get Christopher.

I walked up the three steps that led to the back door and went inside. I heard Whiskey's meow somewhere in the trees, but Mom was already behind me carrying my brother, and she closed the door. Whiskey had never spent the night outside here before. I was already trembling, and worried for her.

There were piles of planks of wood and tools near the back of the house where we parked the cars. It was being used to slowly build a ceiling over the living room. As we entered the kitchen, the living room seemed darker. The ceiling was finished now. Instead of seeing straight up to the peak of the A-Frame house, we were in an almost normal shaped room. It'd still have two walls that were slanted.

My room was no longer downstairs. It was now upstairs where my parents used to sleep. It was like an attic space above the kitchen, bathroom and my old room below. My brother's crib was moved up there too. My parents' bedroom was now in the new space above the living room. So now, in order to get to my room, I had to go through the living room.

As we entered the living room, I went slowly towards the light across the room to turn it on. This house was usually dark because there were only windows on the flat side of the walls. I stopped when I saw a lighter flick on and my eyes adjusted to the shape of my dad. He was in complete shadow. My mom struggled to hold Christopher and find the lamp's switch. As soon as the room lit partially by the lamp, I saw his face quietly staring at us from the lit ashes.

My mom pushed me from behind and I rushed upstairs. Not a word was said, and I was thrust into bed still with my clothes on and tucked in quickly. I lay there in silence. The darkness smothered me to sleep. And the last thing I heard was Whiskey's meow from somewhere outside.

I heard something shatter and I sat up quickly in bed. My heart was already awake. My stomach was pounding in my gut. I grabbed the blankets and held them to my throat.

There were thuds coming from downstairs.

"Oh God, Dean," I heard my mom sob.

My eyes widened, as if that were going to help me see through the night.

There were a few more thuds followed by a roar that sounded like a tornado. I had learnt about tornadoes from *The Wizard of Oz* and Michigan had tornadoes sometimes. They were very loud. If you shouted, you still couldn't hear yourself. It was a bunch of wind and dirt and clouds that twirled together and raced across the ground. In *The Wizard of Oz*, it was so powerful it picked up a whole house and took it to a magical land called Oz. I wished we were being taken to Oz.

I slipped out of bed, but my legs didn't allow me to stand. They were shaking so badly that I sunk to my hands and knees. I crawled to the stairs that led down to the living room. It was absolutely dark, except for a faded light coming from the kitchen. I edged myself down each step with my butt. When I reached the bottom, the thuds and screams and roars were coming from the kitchen. My heart was hurting from the hard beating in my chest. I stood up. My legs threatened to fail, but I stepped off the stairs and stood in front of the couch and looked towards the walkway that led into the kitchen. I could see his shadow. It was darting around the kitchen. A lumped shadow moved from the floor. A single arm lifted up and fell. I knew whose shadow that belonged to.

I tried to call out, "Mom?"

But like my legs, my voice couldn't do its job.

The shadow of my father loomed over my mom's. Its arms lifted up and struck down. I heard the thuds again and my mom's sobs.

My dad was a monster. A terrible, horrible Shadow Monster.

I had left the Sword of Omens upstairs in my room in my toy box. I wished I had it now. I imagined raising The Sword of Omens above my head like Lion-O did with the Thundercats. I imagined using his magic to call a phoenix to my side. I imagined hopping onto a unicorn and running into the kitchen and rescuing my mom and defeating the Shadow Monster.

I imagined saving the day and calling Grandma Boyer like she told us to. I imagined her arriving on her own unicorn and hugging me and telling me that I did a good job. She'd tell me that she always knew I had the strength.

However, my fiery phoenix wasn't strong enough. I couldn't be the hero that I wanted to be. Like the Lion in the Land of Oz, I was a coward.

The Shadow Monster was too strong and too loud and too terrifying. I just watched the shadow against the wall as it continued to hit and throw my mom's shadow around. My legs wouldn't move forward anymore. They wanted to go back up the stairs and so I let them.

I ran back up the stairs. I stumbled into my room. I dived into bed. I covered myself up with my blankets and I cried quietly. I wanted to cry loudly, but I didn't want the monster to hear me. I didn't want to be found. So I closed my eyes tightly. I swallowed the screams that my throat now wanted to make. I forced my heart to beat against my ribs. I soaked my face with my tears and I begged the thuds to stop. I begged the screams to stop. I begged for the monster to go away.

And that's when I heard her. A loud vibration from somewhere beneath my bed. It consumed me. It's all I heard, until I felt the vibration through the bed. I was terrified as the blankets moved away from my face and a softness brushed away my tears. I felt a nudge against my chin and a warmth against my beating heart. My arms wrapped around her quickly.

Whiskey licked my face and meowed quietly. A soft, quick little mew before her purrs filled the space beneath the blankets. She rested her head against my neck. Her front paws slipped on either sides of my neck and her warm belly pressed against my chest. I could feel her heartbeat and now my heart began to match its rhythm.

"I'm happy to have you," I whispered to her.

Whiskey meowed in reply, and I knew exactly what she said back to me. "I'm happy to have you, too."

A Year In Shadow

Thud.

The sound was like an alarm for me each night. My eyes would snap open. I'd hold my breath. I'd listen for the second sound.

Thud.

I'd slide out of my bed and stare at its emptiness. A part of me wanted to get back beneath the covers. I wanted to hide. I wanted to be safe.

Thunk. Thud.

"Oh God, Dean," I'd hear her say sometimes. "Stop it. Please."

Sometimes I wouldn't hear her say anything at all. She'd try to be so quiet like I would be as I took a step down the stairs until the Shadow Monster was seen on the wall. I'd stop and listen. I'd slide down onto my butt and sit there. I'd wince as his fists fell onto my mom's shadow.

Thud. Thwack. Thunk.

I'd feel each hit as if he were hitting me. Silent tears would stream down my face. I couldn't be her hero like I wanted. I couldn't convince my legs to complete the steps and go out into the darkness of the living room to the light of the kitchen. I couldn't take care of her like I was supposed to.

"I'll need you to take care of me," I'd whisper to myself as I remembered my mom's words. But I couldn't. I couldn't go out there. So I sat there instead and winced and cried and watched and listened. I stayed until her shadow fell silent and his shadow lit a cigarette and just stood over her.

When it was silent and the broken air settled, I returned to my bed. I'd lie there and shiver as I stared up into the darkness of the crevice of the triangle house.

Every single night. Every night that happened. And I'd lay there and shove my thumb into my mouth and lay there. I'd stay there till

Whiskey appeared and she'd slide her paws around my neck and hold me. Her purrs would tell me it was all alright now. She was there.

Whiskey was always there.

The morning after I'd walk into the kitchen. I wouldn't say a word. I'd just get the broom or take it from my mom if she was already there. I'd clean up the kitchen with her and then we'd clean her up together. That's when I could take care of her, I learnt quickly. I just couldn't save her. It was hard to focus on anything else at home.

I couldn't focus on school either. It flickered passed me like a dream. All I could see was the Shadow Monster looming around me. In my dreams. In the house. Driving in the car. Smoking. Drinking. Raging. Crying. Making me see things I didn't want to see, but he made me watch. My Batman was gone and I didn't think he was coming back.

I just tried to talk a lot when he wasn't around. I played toys with my brother. I made as many people smile and laugh as I could because when they were smiling and laughing, so was I. I could pretend that nothing was happening. My mom taught me that.

I'd ask her, "Why does Dad hit you at night?"

Her face would go pale at first. She'd struggle with her words, but soon her varied answers were automatic, "It's nothing. It's fine." "Work is getting to him." "He's sick. He'll get better. I'll take care of him." "We're family. We forgive and move on. That's what we will do." "He said he was sorry. It's okay now."

I never. Ever. Liked her answers.

The mornings never went well after the Shadow Monster came. I had to come up with something to make my mom laugh while we cleaned up. I had to get everyone to forget that last night was another night of screaming, thudding and glass breaking.

The Shadow Monster lived there now.

136

I turned 6 that summer and spent it exploring the woods around the A-Frame. Whiskey would follow me around and explore with me. My obsession with cartoons and toys grew bigger, even though Thundercats had ended. I still watched the reruns and had the Super Friends to watch. Toys helped me hide in my room when the yelling would begin or outside when it was still light enough to play. I went anywhere the Shadow Monster wasn't resting and waiting to strike. The yelling with my mom and dad got worse. The mornings became even quieter.

When we went shopping, I would see children picking out clothes for school. They'd chatter about with their parents. I'd see dads with their sons. They'd be smiling or laughing or talking. My dad was silent. He'd be chewing gum or leave the store to go outside and smoke. When he did speak it was with an angry voice about how people were annoying him or how he just wanted to go already. Whenever he drove, he always had wild eyes and the car ride had to be silent or he'd snap. The children I saw with their dads didn't look scared. They didn't look like they felt sick or winced when their father made a quick movement. Every time I saw those families I realised my life wasn't normal. I didn't have a normal family. I wasn't normal. Like my dad said, I was the cursed firstborn. He kept saying it was all my fault and no matter what I did to try to fix myself, it never made it better.

Every day I was scared.

I waited for the bus by myself. I'd watch an older brother and sister exit their house across the road. Their mother was always there to see them off. I wished I were a part of their family. It made me feel so alone. Until one day, the sister waved at me and the brother told me to come stand with them.

At first, I was shy. The fear that always lived in me now almost had me stay in my yard, but I was scared they would wake my father. So I ended up going to keep them quiet. The sister, Emily, was nice and sometimes when I was outside playing with my toys, she'd come over to say hello. Her brother Eric sometimes came over too. His smile made me feel safe and warm.

Emily would smile down at me, reaching out to give me a hug. I'd give her a hug always and I'd give one to Eric too because his reactions always made me laugh.

He'd give a goofy smile, "Boys don't hug," and hug me anyway.

Eric had great hugs. He had strong arms and I felt safe in his embrace.

I'd tell them stories of my toys and the fun adventures I'd have with Whiskey in the woods.

Emily giggled, "You have such a good imagination."

"You just like playing house with him," Eric smirked.

"Oh, please," she stuck her tongue out, "you pretended to be the mom, too."

Eric's mouth dropped open. "Shut up. I was bored. What else were we supposed to do? Play with his baby toys?"

"I like when Eric plays as the mom."

Eric and Emily laughed.

I reached out and held Eric's hand. He looked wide-eyed at Emily but she shook her head, smiled fondly down at me and took my other hand.

Eric would always help me on board the yellow bus. He would put me into one of the front seats and headed to the back of the bus with Emily. My stomach was bouncing around inside of me. I had tried to go back with them, but Emily stopped and pushed me back down.

138

"Little kids sit in the front," she giggled, and continued to follow her brother.

My eyes snapped open. It was starting again but this time my mom started screaming. She only did that if he was getting too bad. Last time that happened, she had to wear a brace on her wrist.

I slid out of bed but as I reached the top of the stairs leading down into the living room, I saw the Shadow Monster move at the bottom of the stairs. I froze. My brain screamed at me to go back into the bed. He could be coming up to see if I were awake. I took a step backwards and the floor creaked. I held my breath. My stomach felt like it was swimming around in my gut. I whimpered.

Music started blaring. The Shadow Monster had turned on the stereo that was next to the television. I watched as he returned back towards the kitchen. I just stood there staring down the emptiness of the stairs.

The song was one of Dad's favourite bands, Tears for Fears, "Shout! Shout! Let it all out! These are the things I can do without!"

I couldn't hear my mom anymore, but I could still hear the roars of his voice as he belted out the song and his fists. I went back to the spot on the stairs and watched the shadows. The song swam heavily inside my head. I covered my ears. I winced in pain as the lyrics kept repeating over and over inside of me. My lips even repeated it sometimes, even if I didn't want them to.

I hated that song. It terrified me and it stopped me from getting out of the bed. It stopped me from being there for my mom. I'd just lay in bed writhing around wanting it all to end. My hands would press so hard against my ears that they'd hurt.

He only played it when he was raging, when the Shadow Monster was fully awake.

I'd curl up in the darkness and cry into Whiskey's fur.

When that song played, I'd be just like my mom and beg, "Oh God, Dean, stop."

These nights repeated more than I could count until one night; there was a loud crash in the kitchen. The music stopped. I heard my mom on the phone.

"Mom, can you get here, please?!" she was begging into the phone.

I knew who she was talking to and I was so hopeful. I hadn't stayed at her place in quite a while. It was always good to see Grandma Boyer.

The Shadow Monster roared, "Oh what is that witch going to do?"

Whiskey hissed towards the stairs leading down to the living room and then purred softly in my ear and licked my face. This was how she tried to take care of me.

"Mom, hurry, please!" my mom howled. She must have hung up the phone because my light turned on and there she was at the top of the stairs. She wasn't surprised I was awake.

"Bring Whiskey," she ordered, her eyes determined as she rocked my crying brother in her arms. "Grandma is on her way."

I sat up with Whiskey in my arms. She didn't fight me as I got up and carried her downstairs. I didn't bother getting dressed. I followed my mom downstairs and through the living room. It was torn apart, but my mom didn't stop. We rushed through the kitchen. The Shadow Monster was there. His shadow wrapped around what used to be my dad. I couldn't look at him anymore.

"Oh YES! You think you're such a big man, DON'T YOU?" he screamed at me.

I could smell his drink.

He tried to come towards me, but my mom screamed at him to stop and then screamed at me to leave. I ran outside with Whiskey in my arms.

"Don't you dare, Dean!" my mom screamed. "I have your son in my arms!"

I looked back just quickly enough to see my mom follow me out and a howl came from the house. "Ruthann, please…pleeeease…don't leave me!"

We rushed down the driveway around the house to the dirt road where I waited for the bus in the morning. We stood there listening to the Shadow Monster screaming and roaring inside. We also heard the sounds of things shattering. It happened so much I imagined the house being completely destroyed inside.

A car pulled into the driveway and out popped Grandma Boyer. My mom rushed to her, but my grandma came straight over to me.

"Michael," she sighed, running a soft hand along my face. "Are you okay, my peanut?"

I nodded, "I have Whiskey."

Grandma Boyer scratched Whiskey behind the ear. "Despite myself I have missed this creature. Take her in the car. When she gets to my house, Whiskey has some rodents to kill."

She shuddered just mentioning them and I sort of smiled at her fear. I walked towards her car. As I tried to get into it, I turned to see Grandma Boyer rocking my crying brother. "Hush, you poor thing. You poor thing. Grandma's here."

She turned from my mom and came back to the car where I still stood.

"Get in the car, Michael," she ordered quietly as she opened the door and both of us winced as we heard crashing from inside the house. I crawled into the car with Whiskey quiet in my arms. I went to put her down on the car seat but she refused to leave my embrace. My grandma noticed and smiled as she locked me into the seatbelt while holding my brother. My mom was right behind her, watching us quietly.

"Can they stay with you for a few days?" she asked Grandma Boyer.

"Yes, you can."

"No, just them."

141

Grandma Boyer scowled. "Oh, no, you're coming too. Get in the car, Ruthann."

My mom shook her head.

"Don't do this. Not again," my grandma hissed. "He won't change. You need to think about your sons and yourself."

"He loves me," my mom now sobbed. "He's just lost so much."

"You all have lost so much," my grandma exclaimed, raising her hands in the air. "Don't do this. You *do* this, and I can't help you. You know? Get in the car and think about your family!"

My mom took a step backwards. "He's my best friend. He needs me. I need him. I can help him."

Grandma Boyer stood her ground. Her glasses slipping to the tip of her nose. "Ruthann, you must put your children first. Always."

"Oh really, mom?" my mom snapped. "Like you did when my brothers --"

Grandma Boyer put a hand up. Her shoulders dropped in defeat. "Fine. I've made my mistakes too. You need to make yours, I see. Fine. You've made your bed. Now lie in it."

After putting my brother into the car seat next to me, she hopped into the driver's seat. She started the car and I suddenly understood what they were talking about. My mom wasn't coming. She was going back into the house. I went to scream for her to come with us.

I wanted us to all be safe but sirens now screamed down the dirt road and into our driveway. Blue and red lights flashed across our yard.

"Don't worry, peanut, I called them," my grandma reassured me as she got back out of the car, leaving it running, and rushed over to the police. She spoke to them quickly before getting back into the car and reversed it onto the road.

When we were safely tucked into bed back in my Grandma Boyer's house, I let out a huge breath as if I hadn't been breathing all year. I finally felt safe. We waited for my mom to come that night. My Grandma Boyer sat with me in bed, holding me tightly against her. But my mom never came. We didn't see her for days.

Every day I'd ask Grandma Boyer, "When is my mom coming?"

And every time she'd push her lips together tightly and say, "I don't know. She's taking care of your father."

"Doesn't she want to take care of us?" I'd ask.

Grandma Boyer would peer down at me through her glasses and run her fingers through my bangs, "I'll take care of you, Michael. All of you."

I loved waking up at Grandma Boyer's house. I always had a nice feeling when I woke up there and could hear her in the kitchen making breakfast. Christopher would always be out there being fed and babbling happily. The mornings were so different here. The house was brighter. My grandma would be humming her usual songs. The house was loud and full of life. The Shadow Monster couldn't live here.

Whiskey was different here, too. She'd relax more and sprawl herself out. She'd be okay with leaving my side and sleeping in. She hated the mornings anyways. I knew she forced herself to get up when we were at the A-Frame. She'd go outside with me there and stay outside until I got home. At Grandma Boyer's house, she had a different job and that was in the garage.

It had been a few days since leaving the A-Frame. I woke up to Grandma's pancakes. I could smell them. I could hear the clanking in the kitchen of pans and spoons. I could hear my grandma and my brother singing and cooing. As I walked out of the room and into the kitchen, Christopher was sitting up in an old metal highchair. His face was smeared with food.

Grandma Boyer saw me and came over. She pushed my hair off my forehead and kissed it. She nodded towards the living room and then to the kitchen. "Hurry up and eat your breakfast. I need to spend the day beating you badly at Chutes and Ladders."

But we didn't get to go play any games because the gravel in the driveway crunched as a car pulled in. It was my parents. I followed my Grandma Boyer to the front door. She slowly opened it. As my mom approached, I could see a bruise on her face. I wanted to ask her who took care of her cuts and bruises but my dad was waiting in the car.

"Time to go," my mom said. "Go get Whiskey, Mike."

I did what I was told and found myself crawling into the car. My mom put Christopher in the back with me. My dad seemed to be overly happy. He made jokes. He laughed at them. He tried to explain things but I couldn't listen. The sound of his voice terrified me and all I could hear was that song he kept playing when he was angry. I just quietly played with Christopher and watched Mom out of the corner of my eye.

We went home to drop Whiskey off and then my dad exclaimed, "Everyone back into the car. I have a surprise for you!"

We obeyed him.

We went out to the ice-cream parlour, the only one in Coleman on the main street. My dad ordered me Superman ice cream, though I didn't want that flavour. I liked pistachio now. I licked at it anyway. He ordered for everyone else as well. The person behind the counter was laughing and grinning at my dad's charm. If I could, I would have told the man to be careful. Beneath that smile was a terrible secret. A shadow.

When we walked out with our ice cream and headed to an empty picnic table, my dad suddenly snapped, "Aren't you going to say thank you? I'm trying here, you know?"

I sat up rigid and choked on my ice cream as if I had taken too big of a bite and quickly said, "Thank you. I like it. It's Superman. It's my favourite."

My dad lit a cigarette and looked pleased with himself. I watched him quietly, while licking my ice cream. I couldn't taste it anymore. My chest felt too heavy. My stomach felt sick. My face felt twisted as my eyebrows grew heavy and my lip curled.

I dropped my ice cream onto the table. My hand just let it go. I stared at my dad with wide eyes as he jumped off the bench yelling, "Damn it, Mike!"

His hands slammed down on the table.

He grabbed napkins and threw them down on the table and ranted a bunch of words that I didn't hear. I couldn't hear. I was too busy watching him. I was too busy feeling the twisted mess that was my stomach.

When we returned to the A-Frame, Whiskey was running around the yard chasing something in the long grass. She called out to me to come play. I stepped towards her but my dad's hand on my shoulder stopped me.

"No," he said, "get inside. We're going to have a talk."

My mom had already gone into the house with Christopher. She was setting him up for dinner as my father led me to the living room. He stood in front of me and slowly took his belt off and folded it up in his hands.

I began to cry. I didn't understand. He had just taken me for ice cream and I know I didn't thank him straight away and I know I dropped it, but he scared me.

He slapped his belt against his hand and towered over me, "I think you need a reminder with manners, son."

I winced each time he hit his hand with his belt. He got closer and closer to me with each slap. When he was towering over me, he twirled me around. When I tried to turn back to look at him, he roughly turned my head to face the other way again.

"No," he growled, "face forward. You need to learn."

I stood there trembling. I fought the urge to look behind me. I could see his shadow move along the floor as he lifted up his arm that held the belt. I wanted to look to see if Mom was going to stop him or if

Christopher was watching. But I didn't move. I just cried. I watched the shadow as it jerked down quickly and a loud smack filled my ears.

I screamed, but I felt no pain. I moved away, knowing I might get in trouble, and spun around. My dad was laughing. He was grinning ear to ear as he held the belt together in his hands. He had not hit me. He had only snapped the belt to make that terrible sound. He had tricked me, and I hated it. I just wanted to get away.

"Go outside now until we call you in for dinner," my mom said.

"I don't know why he's blubbering like a baby," he continued chuckling. "I didn't hit him. My dad did worse to my brother and sisters and I when we were kids."

"Wait," he said and went upstairs where they were still working on their new room. I stood at the front door with my mother, who didn't look at me. He walked back into the kitchen from the living room and hammered a nail into the wall. He hung up his belt on the nail.

"Dean," my mom warned.

"There," he snapped, "Let that be a reminder to how much worse it could be."

The door to the A-Frame closed behind me and I stood there staring at the browning grass. I watched the leaves slowly fall to the ground. I felt like the world around me. Summer was ending and soon the cold chill of winter would begin. I already felt it. I ran towards the woods unsure of where I was going. I just knew I had to get away from the house.

Soon, thick fluffy snow covered the ground. In the mornings when the sun reflected off of it, it would blind me. That was only if it weren't actually snowing. Blizzards made the days grey. If it was fine and there was lots of snow on the ground, we would spend our days sledding or building snow forts. Christopher was still too little to stay out for too long. My dad only played occasionally if we were home at the A-Frame on our own, and not with my mom's family.

Eventually, the snow would make my clothes soaking wet. My eyes would sting from the cold and my chest would hurt. Sometimes it would snow so heavily I couldn't go outside. I'd have to worry about staying out of my dad's way if he were up or staying quiet when he was asleep.

Or it was so cold that it was almost as if winter was indoors too. We'd always have to dress warm and have the heat on. My mom and dad would complain about the ice on the roads and how dangerous it was. They'd tell stories of the car spinning around or getting stuck in a snowdrift and they'd have to dig their way out.

I just walked silently through the kitchen and into the living room. I stood at the front glass door that led out to the front yard. The belt rattled against its nail on the wall. Ever since my dad put his belt on the nail, it was used often.

I knew when it was going to be used, too. His eyes would flicker with signs of the Shadow Monster.

He'd point to the living room floor and growl, "Lie down."

I walked to the same spot he always pointed to and dropped to the floor.

"On your belly," he growled again, but I was so used to this that I had already gotten onto my belly. I was already trembling.

"Arms and legs spread."

I spread them. I could smell the floor. I could hear the belt come off the nail. My eyes snapped shut and I clenched my teeth together. If I didn't, I might have bit my tongue. I did that once.

"You think because you're the firstborn you can do whatever you want. You think you run this house. You think I want to do this? I don't want to deal with you!"

His voice was getting louder and louder and that's when I heard the snap. At first, I just flinched. The Shadow Monster loved scaring me and then a fire spread up my legs. It was in a row from my left ankle up my calf over to my right thigh. The snap happened again. Fire this time on my back. Snap. Snap. Snap. Fire spread across my shoulders, my arms, my backside.

Sometimes, if I squeezed my eyes tight enough, I could imagine the nights the Shadow Monster hit my mom. I'd hear the thuds instead of the snaps.

I screamed but no one ever heard me. Even if they did, no one ever saved me.

When March 5th, 1987 Happened

As spring settled around us, my brother and I were moved back into the small room right across from the bathroom. I was glad to be further from my dad. I hated trying to tiptoe down the stairs as he slept behind a thin wall. Even if we made the stairs creak, he'd wake up and yell that we were too loud. And the fighting no longer happened in the kitchen, it happened in the living room.

The worst part was during the mornings when we had to quietly walk through the kitchen if our dad was already awake. Luckily for us, that rarely happened. He still slept throughout the day and worked at night. When he wasn't working, we had no idea what his schedule was going to be. Usually we were already in the living room watching cartoons. Besides, when he woke up, the TV was turned off and we were sent outside. I didn't mind. I had my brother and we had our toys. Sometimes, we'd even go exploring in the woods together, but I'd always walk too fast and he'd call to me to wait up. I usually had to wait for Whiskey to catch up, too.

My brother and I sat in the grass area between the trees of the woods and the dirt driveway that looped around the A-Frame. The grass was starting to wake up from its slumber.

Christopher was banging two toys together as they battled it out. I was more interested in the dialogue that was happening between the heroes and villains of mine. Captain America and Hawkman were fighting against Mumm-Ra. They had almost killed my GI Joe toy dressed as a hawk, too. They'd eventually fight, but the same side didn't always win.

When I watched cartoons like Thundercats, the heroes always won and the show would end with all of them laughing. I loved those stories and I wanted them to be true. But here I was six, going on seven, sitting in my yard trying to play as loud as I could to cover the music my dad was blaring in the house. He was listening to Cream.

I had learnt that the bad guys won sometimes. When I watched my two-year-old brother play, he always had the good guys win, too. Sometimes I made him cry when I would have the bad guys win. I

149

didn't mean to make him cry, and I promised him the next time, the good guys would win. I learnt that if my stories were going to end unhappily ever after, I had to give some hope for the good guys or else other people got upset. Like my brother.

My brother was talking more and more. I loved it. I taught him the names of all the superheroes. I helped him to read, even though it was mostly pointing at pictures and naming what he saw. He didn't really know what words meant. We would sit on the couch together, much like how my dad and I used to sit, and Christopher would clap his hands and giggle madly when I was proud of him getting a name or a colour right. Our favourite books were The Monster At The End of This Book and Because A Little Bug That Went Ka-Choo.

One afternoon when my brother and I were playing, my mom told us she was expecting a baby. We didn't know whether we were getting a brother or sister, but I knew I would have to take care of them, too.

"Christopher," I said to him as he banged the toys together, "Do you remember Arizona?"

"No," he said, and then continued making fighting noises.

"I do. It was okay. I like it here better because it's so green. The grass is so soft and all the flowers and trees are lovely. There's more animals, too," I said as I flipped the toy I was holding into the air. This figure was dressed as a hawk so I pretended he was flying. "You didn't like Arizona. You hated the heat. You'd get all red and sweaty, and cry a lot. I helped take care of you, though. But we lost our hopes and dreams there, I think."

Christopher lifted up his hands holding the two toys and shrugged. "What's that?"

"Dad once told me about hopes and dreams," I said. "I think we had some of them, but we lost them. We had a big house with a pool. We had nice things. Dad had a motorcycle."

"Vrooom?" Christopher asked.

"Yeah," I nodded, "Dad vroomed all over the place. Our Grandpa and Grandma Stoneburner are still back there. You don't remember, but they really loved music and would sing all the time. Grandpa played a banjo and would sing. Grandma had a tambourine and she's sing too. She had the best hugs."

"Where are they?" he asked in his little voice. His voice was as chubby as his cheeks.

"They're still in Arizona," I said. I looked over at the house as the music stopped. I wondered if Mom was going to let us go back inside soon.

"You won't remember, but there was this one time in Arizona, I tried to help you out of the crib. You were crying and wanted to get out and play. Mom was at work and Dad was in the living room, being sad. He had to get rid of his motorbike."

"Vrooom!" my brother said again, pretending his two toys were now motorbikes.

"I reached up to pull you out and you flipped over, and we both went crashing to the floor."

Christopher stopped playing and listened to me. He loved my stories.

"We both fell backwards, and I thought you would bounce because you were really chubby."

He bounced up and down in the grass. "Boing. Boing. Boing."

I giggled, "No. You didn't bounce. I panicked. You were screaming. I think you were hurt and I was so worried. I dashed out of your room and ran to tell Dad. But he heard the crash and came running. Just as I was running out, Dad was running in. We didn't see each other, and we crashed together. Boom!"

Christopher slammed his two toys together and made a crashing sound.

"Dad was like a speeding train. I wasn't, though. I was tiny compared to him. I went flying like Superman, into the wall. I felt as though I flew up into the ceiling first, so I bet you I did. And then I hit the wall. Actually, I bet you I hit the ceiling, and then the wall, then the floor and back to the wall again. Boing. Boing Boing."

We both made the noises together and we bounced around in the grass and laughed like hyenas.

151

When we settled down, I looked back at the A-Frame. The house was silent now, and sometimes the silence scared me as much as the loud noises did. I stood up and wiped the grass and dirt off of me. I gathered my toys and picked up the bottom of my shirt and used it as a pouch. I started walking towards the house with Christopher following me. He was still making bouncing noises and laughing. I neared the back door and stopped. Something was wrong. I felt it. I looked back at Christopher who was still trying to catch up. When he did, the back door opened, and my mom peeked out.

She peered over at the yard and shouted, "Mike! Christopher! WHERE --"

"Mom, we're right here," I laughed.

She looked down at us startled, and I could see panic in her eyes.

"I need you to get your brother in the car, Michael. Put away your toys. We have to go."

I felt a tightness in my stomach, but I nodded and went inside.

We both threw our toys on the beds and went back outside to the car. My mom had gone upstairs and was talking to my dad. It took her awhile going up and down the stairs. She was pregnant now. It was the reason I was moved downstairs with my brother. Our old crib was upstairs where I used to sleep, waiting for our new brother or sister to be born. We were waiting for it to be a surprise.

We were sitting in the back of the car before I was brave enough to ask, "Where are we going?"

"We're going to your grandma's house," she said quickly, and leaned over and honked the horn. My dad came out of the house and shrugged.

"I was looking for my lighter," he said before he slowly made his way to the driver's seat.

"Dean, come on," my mom pleaded. She was worried about something.

For my mom, the drive seemed to take forever, but not for my brother and me. We always played games together. We got to do more stuff

152

together now that he could talk and understand things. He even loved playing Chutes and Ladders. I'd win most of the time.

"Cheater," he'd pretend to pout, and then smile a bit.

"I am not," I said, holding my nose in the air like Grandma Boyer had taught me. "I use my resources."

"What is that?" my brother would always ask, shrugging his shoulders.

I'd just laugh.

"You okay, Mom?" I asked her as we neared Grandma's house.

"Your grandma is sick," she said. Her legs were tapping against the car floor.

"Did she see a mouse again?" I asked.

Once I had been with my mom in Grandma's living room when I heard her scream from in the garage. I never saw her run so quickly out the front door. Down the driveway. Passed the mailbox. Her screams echoing across the sky. This made Mom and I laugh, but when she returned, she threatened to whip us both with a branch from the Willow Tree. Both of us stopped laughing quickly and that's when Grandma Boyer would laugh at us.

When we arrived to Grandma Boyer's house, and before dad could park the car around all the other vehicles in the driveway, mom had opened her door already. There were so many people at the front door. Were they waiting for us?

When we all got out of the car and headed to the front door, my brother and I stayed back a bit. We didn't want to get trampled. Grandpa Boyer walked over to us and flipped his dentures in his mouth. It always made us laugh. He reached behind our ears and found a penny before giving each of us one.

He winked at me, "Try not to swallow these pennies. No-one is going to go through your poo for these."

We laughed before he took a deep breath and walked back over to the other adults. I followed and started to ask what was going on, but I didn't have time to ask questions. I didn't have time to talk. I didn't have time to do anything. It was hard for me not to be able to talk or do anything. I have to talk. I have to do stuff. It was a rule.

We went to the hospital. I understood it was where people went to get better if they were sick but I didn't know why we were there. It smelled cold and there were many rooms with many people in beds. I didn't like it there, and I wanted to know why we were there. I quickly found out when we entered one of the rooms where Grandma Boyer lay in a bed. Her glasses were off. I tried to find her glasses, but I couldn't.

"How is she supposed to see?" I asked loudly, but my mom told me to stay quiet. She had taken Christopher and me by the hand and we went into the room while everyone went out. I didn't know where Dad had gone. I didn't understand why no one else could come in. We had to stand really close to Grandma's bed. Her skin was yellow.

"Why is her skin yellow?" I asked, but my mom quieted me again. For some reason, we weren't allowed to talk in the hospital. When I wandered around the room, my mom hissed at me to come back to the bedside, even though I didn't want to. I didn't want to see Grandma Boyer this way.

I couldn't talk. I couldn't do anything.

"I don't want a fuss." Grandma Boyer's voice suddenly broke the silence.

My mom was in tears, "What's happening?"

"Oh, don't you worry about it," my Grandma Boyer tried to wave her away, "I don't want you upsetting the baby."

"Why didn't you tell anyone?" my mom asked her.

Grandma Boyer pointed to a bedside table with a gift and a card on it. "That's for you. Make sure you take it with you when you leave. Don't open it till after the baby is born."

"Give it to me yourself when that happens," my mom sobbed.

"Oh, you know me," my grandma tried to wave my mom's tears off. "I'd forget."

"No, you wouldn't," my mom said.

154

I stepped up to the bed. My grandma reached a hand out and stroked my face and moved the hair out of my eyes. She smiled at me and went to speak, but closed her mouth quickly. Her eyes looked like they were burning.

I didn't get to stay in the room long after that. Grandma Boyer asked to speak with my mom alone and after that the nurses had to take care of her and no one was allowed back into her room

After visiting the hospital, we went back to Grandma's house. Everyone was quiet. Christopher and I were sent to bed. I curled up in the bunk bed I was used to sleeping in, but something was different. The house wasn't the same without Grandma. Dad had gone back home. Mom spent the evening quietly with her sister. There were so many adults around, and each disappeared at different times. Not one of them approached me and told me what was going on. I didn't understand.

I waited for Grandma Boyer to come home. She'd explain everything. She wouldn't make me wait.

I just waited. In that room. On that bed.

Morning came slowly. I was awake before dawn. I lay there listening to my brother's little snores. He didn't know what was going on either, and when he asked, I couldn't answer and I hated not knowing.

I hadn't seen Grandma Boyer as much as I used to see her. There was always an excuse, but I knew it was because my dad didn't like her. She would always stand up to him and they'd get into arguments. Now, as the sun rose, all I wanted to do was see her. I wanted to walk out of the bedroom and see her cooking us pancakes. I wanted to play board games and sing songs.

The door opened and I grinned. I imagined it was Grandma Boyer grinning at me. Telling me that she tricked me. It was just pretend. She'd nod her head to make me follow her. I'd smell her delicious breakfast.

But it wasn't her. It was a couple of my aunts. They sat with me. It was like when I wanted to speak when my mouth was full. I wasn't sure why but the looks they gave each other told me I didn't want to

155

hear what they had to say, but they said it. I could see each word caused them pain as they both tried to explain what was going on. They almost couldn't do it. But they did. One gave me a hug. That one hug that I still feel to this day when I just don't understand what's happening in my world. Their voices soon just mixed together in my head. I couldn't tell which one was talking anymore.

I couldn't tell which one told me that Grandma Boyer was dead.

The Gift of Foresight

Sometimes when I went to church with Grandma Boyer, I'd hear about heaven and God and hell. Heaven was a place good people went to. Hell was a place bad people went to. I don't know why but all those times I heard it explained to me didn't matter. I just listened to the words and accepted that's how it was and would always be. I didn't know what it meant.

I wished I were in church with my grandma now. I'd ask her more questions. I closed my eyes and let the tears come. I imagined her stroking my face and moving the hair out of my eyes so she could kiss my forehead. Again, I imagined the front door opening and Grandma telling me it was all a trick for the times I laughed when a mouse scared her. She would wave her hand for me to come out of my room so we could play Chutes and Ladders. She'd win, of course and I'd tell her she cheated. She'd shake her head and say that she was just using her resources. Christopher would be there shrugging his shoulders, asking us both what that meant.

But none of that ever happened, no matter how much I imagined it.

The days blurred together. So many people came and went in Grandma's house. Grandpa Boyer was already packing up the house and this was upsetting my mom. I felt like I was standing in an empty room as people just zoomed past me, running as fast as The Flash.

I'd see Grandma Boyer one more time after that, in a building where people sat in wooden seats crying. I tried to understand it all. The funeral home seemed a lot like a church but this place was just for people to get together and be sad. There were so many people. I stayed close to my mom. There were many people I recognised as part of the family, but the others were just blurs. Some people were asking my mom to have me wait outside and that's when I realised there weren't other kids around. It was just me. Were children not allowed in the funeral home? I tried asking my mom but I could see in her eyes that she was just as lost as I felt. She kept pushing me forwards through the small room that had flowers and a person welcoming us inside and apologising to us for our loss.

"Mike," she said to me as we walked up the aisle of the funeral home, "This is your chance to say goodbye."

I stayed silent. I wasn't doing much talking these days. I just sat around and ate, or I watched the adults quietly as they rushed around. In the back of the room my mom was taking me through was a big box. It had a lid open and steps leading up to it. It was low enough for me to already see that someone was sleeping inside of it. It was almost as if I was walking up to where Snow White slept waiting for her handsome prince to come.

But it wasn't Snow White. The sleeping person looked like my Grandma Boyer, but it wasn't. There was a small stair put alongside the coffin. It was for me. The other adults could just lean over. I had to step closer to the body. I looked down at the face that seemed so smooth. She looked like one of my plastic action figures. I was told I wasn't allowed to touch her, but I didn't want to anyway. I didn't know why everyone was telling me this was her. She wasn't there. I couldn't feel her.

This Grandma Boyer wasn't feisty.

"Good bye, Mom." My mom sobbed into a tissue and walked away, leaving me alone with her. I looked down one more time before I turned away. No one was near me. Everyone else was off crying. I didn't know what to do. I couldn't cry. I had already done all that. I just wanted to go home. I just wanted to hold Whiskey and play toys with my brother.

An organ played some music that echoed in my chest. It felt like sadness. People were finding a seat and I was just standing in the front, lost.

I imagined my Grandma Boyer walking over to me. It's what she would do if she were here. She wouldn't leave me on my own. She would make sure I was taken care of, and she'd explain things to me. I imagined her taking me by the hand and looking down at the sleeping person. "You're right, Mike. That's not me. I think this place has some old board games in a cupboard. How about we have a round of Sorry?"

But my wish didn't come true no matter how hard I imagined it. I would not be playing board games with Grandma Boyer again. I stepped off the stairs and wished I were following my grandma back to where my mom was sitting instead of finding my own way alone. I sat down next to Mom. She didn't seem to notice.

The day disappeared. Words were said about my grandma. Kind words, until no one could talk anymore. Just like me. That's when everyone went home.

My mom was sitting at the kitchen table when I came out of my room. When we had arrived home, I disappeared inside where Christopher was already playing toys. Whiskey was asleep on the bed curled up on a quilt Grandma Boyer had made. It wasn't finished, and Grandpa Boyer was going to it throw away, but it was saved and given to my mom.

I quietly walked up to mom. She was rubbing her belly, where a new baby was growing. She was holding the wrapped present from beside Grandma's hospital bed. It was wrapped like a birthday present but it wasn't for any of our birthdays.

I rested my head against her arm, and placed my hand on her belly. I did like to feel the baby kick. Every time I touched Mom's belly, the baby kicked me, or gave me a high five. I knew the baby already liked me.

"This present is from your Grandma Boyer," she said as if she had forgotten I was there when it was given to her. "It's the last thing she gave to me. She told me to open it later. It's for the baby."

"I miss her," I whispered.

"Me too," she sighed, and kissed my forehead, "Let's open it."

I nodded. I didn't want to say that Grandma had told her to wait. She needed to open it. Her hands trembled as she opened the envelope and pulled out a card.

She opened the card and read it to me. "To my daughter, for your little girl."

My mom dropped her head and cried. I held my mom and cried with her. Through her tears she kept repeating, "How does she know? We don't even know if it is a boy or girl. How does she know?"

She tore at the paper wrapped around the gift. There was a small pink baby's bib inside and some clothing.

Grandma Irene Marie Boyer went to heaven. Two months later, my little sister, Christina Marie, was born. The last thing my grandma did was just a little bit naughty and a little bit feisty. My mom and dad wanted it to be a surprise about whether it would be a boy or a girl, but Grandma Boyer ruined the surprise. I love her.

Mrs. Eden

Turning 7 felt empty. I'd watch television and movies and see children having birthdays with tons of friends and tons of family, but not my birthdays. I never had any friends over. We no longer went out and the Boyer family was never around anymore. The Stoneburner family were still all in Arizona. My birthday only reminded me just how different I was to everyone else.

Soon fall was starting to show around the A-Frame but it never did seem like a summer vacation for me anyway. The deep green was beginning to fade but my world faded back in March. I didn't want to start a new school year at the end of a year where I lost one of my best friends. I didn't let Whiskey leave my side that summer and it wasn't like we left the house anyway. My mom grew quieter, putting all of her voice on my dad, my new sister and going back to work or school or whatever it was she was doing now. I couldn't keep track. All I knew is that she grew more and more angry with the Boyer family. She said it was because they were all forgetting Grandma Boyer already and that made me angry with them too. Why would anyone want to forget her? She was the best.

I did a lot of things on my own now. Waiting for the bus was one of them. Eric and Emily no longer rode with me. They'd wave at me as their car drove past. I wished they'd give me a ride.

At Coleman Elementary, I weeded through the waves of kids and parents. I remembered when Grandma Boyer would take me or I'd go to her house after school. That felt like such a long time ago.

Mrs. Eden was the name of my second grade teacher. She was standing at the door saying hello to her new students. I thought I was doing fine that morning until I saw her at the door. That's when my stomach starting fluttering. I worried about Jason mucking up in her class or Kyle and her friends talking through her lessons. When Mrs. Eden saw me, she grinned and my worry faded. She was in a flowered dress full of reds and purples and whites. Her hair was short, curly and grey. She had wrinkles as she smiled down at me.

"Welcome back," Mrs. Eden said. "So who are we?"

"Mike," I said shyly.

"Mike? Michael? Or is it Mikey? Or Mister Potato Head?"

I giggled.

"It's young Mister Giggles, is it? Well, I'm doomed already. I didn't write young Mister Giggles on your desk. I put Mike, so that will have to do. Is that okay?"

I giggled again and nodded. She gave me a big hug before patting me into her room. Her hug seemed so warm and so inviting. It almost reminded me of Grandma Boyer's hugs.

As the crowd in the hall faded and the bell started the day, Mrs. Eden walked into the classroom and closed the door. "All right, are we all inside? Time to start the day, and I'm going to need your help."

Colourful posters hung up around the room. Some had superheroes on them. There were no Alphas. There was a corner labelled Reading Corner, where there were books for us to read. Our desks each had a little paper bag with our name on it, but we wouldn't even sit at our desks until much later in the day. When I eventually got to my seat, I'd open it up to see that it was lollies for us to take home.

"Jason," I said as he sat in his desk, "get up. We aren't sitting down yet."

Jason rolled his eyes at me and stood up behind his desk. "I get it. The Pledge of Allegiance."

I had already hung up my bag in my own personal cupboard. It still had my name on it from earlier that year. Other students were still looking for theirs.

"Jason," I said as he just stood there with his bag at his feet, "You need to go put your bag in your cupboard. I can help you find it."

"I can do it myself," he huffed, picking up his bag and walking past me.

"Did you have a good summer?" I asked, but he just walked passed me to the bag area.

I listened as other students were talking about their summers. Some of them had hung out together. Others had gone away on vacations to Disney World or Disneyland. I watched as some students boasted about having new bags and clothes. I decided to stay quiet. I just didn't feel like talking.

"Quickly come to the rug and let's talk about what we have done since the last day of school to our first day of second grade!" Mrs. Eden smiled as she clasped her hands together.

I always thought it was confusing talking about the last day of school in May when the last day of the year was December, but that's when it was the middle of the school year. In Australia, they started their school at the beginning of the year and ended around Christmas. That made more sense to me.

We all gathered onto a rainbow rug that was placed in front of a big red chair where Mrs. Eden sat. She opened up a book and began to read aloud. I loved listening to her. She did the voices for each character when they spoke. When we laughed and snorted, she didn't tell us to be quiet. By the end of the story, we were all awake, and ready to start the day. She'd have us stand right where we were seated and recite the Pledge of Allegiance. The way she had us say it, it was almost like a song. It made me smile.

After the pledge, she had us do some stretches while she brought out math cards we had to read with her, and a song we had to sing to help learn our numbers. There were no pencil holders. I didn't have to worry about where I put my hands, or if being me was okay. I just focused on each lesson.

As I sat on the rainbow carpet I noticed there was a gap between me and the other students. I looked around. Mark wasn't there. There was only one Second Grade class, so he must have missed school today, or perhaps he'd moved away. Eric was sitting in the back with Jason. They were playing around with something and I shook my head at them. Mrs. Eden was nice. They should be paying attention. Kyle was sitting next to Vicky and a girl named Tabitha. I couldn't see Amanda either. There were a few more students I saw that I didn't recognise. They must have been new, as they weren't really sitting next to anyone. I was near the front.

It wasn't till after lunch that we finally sat at our desks. I liked the way Mrs. Eden arranged the desks. It was different. Her desks were in groups. We had table points. We were to work together to get these points, and, if we did, we would get a prize.

Across from me sat Tabitha. Next to me sat Eric. Across from him was Kyle. Vicky was sitting in a group on the other side of the room, so she and Kyle had a moment of hugs and goodbyes. I raised one of my eyebrows. They would still be in the room. It wasn't like one of them went to heaven.

"Hi, Kyle," I said when she sat back down after her tearful farewell.

She tried to smile. "Hi, Mikey."

I frowned. I didn't want to be called that.

"Now I want your group to get to know each other," Mrs. Eden said to the class. "Ask each other questions, and when I ring this bell," she added, holding up a small handheld bell, "I want you to stop. Then I'm going to come around and ask each of you about the other people at your table."

Kyle went first. She talked about where she got her name. I liked hearing this story about how her uncle had died in the war and she was born soon after. It made me think of my sister.

"Hey, my sister's middle name is my Grandma Boyer's middle name! My mom says my sister's name is also like Christ In A Mary. Christina Marie. Get it?" I added. "I was named after two of my uncles. My first name and my middle name!"

"It's not your turn, Mikey," Eric snapped.

"Wait a minute," I gasped, "Is that why your hair is short, too? To be like your uncle?"

Eric covered his mouth and snickered. Tabitha looked at me as if I'd done something rude.

"What? My dad was in the army and he had to shave his head, but he didn't like it and got sick."

Kyle glared at me and crossed her arms. Her big blue eyes were still glaring at me while Eric continued laughing.

"Some boys have long hair," Tabitha said next to me, and smiled over at Kyle.

"Yeah," Kyle said. "And stop laughing, Eric, or I'm telling."

"I used to have blonde hair like yours," I said to Kyle, "but my dad shaved it off and it grew back brown."

"It did not," Eric replied.

"It did," I said. "I have photos to prove it."

"Did you ever want to change your boy's name to a girl's?" I asked. I couldn't wait to share with the rest of the class about Kyle's unique name.

"No!" Kyle exclaimed and sat up straight.

I had upset her and I didn't mean to.

I went to say sorry but Kyle suddenly said, changing the subject, "Eric, where did you get your lunch tin and why do you use it for your pencils and not lunch?"

I looked at his lunch tin for the first time and put my hands up to my lips, "It's a superhero one! That's Captain America. That's Spider-Man."

He grinned and held it up. "My dad got it for me for my birthday. I'm eight, so he bought eight pencils to put inside of it. I have a really big pencil, too. Want to see it?"

We nodded our heads eagerly and I blurted, "I'm only seven. I hope I get that for my birthday. I have a Disney one. It's in my bag. I got some GI Joe toys, but I lost one in the yard. He had a hawk costume on. I lost him the day my grandma got-"

"Mikey," Kyle frowned, "It's Eric's turn to speak."

I clapped my hands together and nodded.

Eric was small for an eight-year-old. He was almost as tiny as my brother. He had blonde hair like I used to have before my dad stole it. He also wore glasses like my mom. He loved superheroes as much as I loved them. I wondered if he had many toys.

Eric held up a large pencil. It was huge and barely fit in his hand. I could easily pretend it was the Sword of Omens.

I sighed, pretending to reach towards his pencil. I imagined myself being Lion-O when he lost the Sword of Omens. He would call to it and it would come to him. I imagined the Iceman pencil doing the same, "Pencil of Omens, come to my hand."

"You're weird," Eric said and the girls laughed.

I laughed too and joked, "It's almost bigger than you!"

The girls looked quietly at Eric, who had a smile while showing us his pencil but it faded. Eric tried to shove the pencil into his tin and started to share the same look Kyle had. He glared at me. "I am not tiny!"

"Well, not as tiny as my brother," I added, sitting up normally. "You're a little bit taller. He's four. He'll be five in January."

Eric slammed back into his seat and crossed his arms just like Kyle was doing. I chewed on my bottom lip.

I turned to Tabitha, who was still looking at me like I was weird.

"Were you really blonde when you were little?" she asked me.

I nodded and looked around the room. There were more blondes, a couple of kids with black hair and a few more that were brown like me. Our class mostly had blonde hair.

"Most of the kids have blonde hair in our class. I wish I still had blonde hair," I said, and reached out and touched one of her pigtails.

Tabitha's pigtails were perfect. They were so tight, and they looked extremely smooth. I had never been this close before. I wanted to see just how soft they were.

Tabitha jumped and jerked her head away from me as I ran my hand down one of her pigtails. My hand was wrapped around it so when she pulled away I tugged at it by mistake.

"Ow!" she cried, "Don't pull my hair!"

"Sorry," I said, trying to rub at the pigtail to make it feel better.

She squealed and shooed me away. I put my hands on my desk and apologised again.

Mrs. Eden walked over to our table, "And what's all the excitement happening here?

Eric, Kyle and Tabitha all spoke at once and they were talking about me.

"He said I have a boy's name and I should change it to a girl's."

"He said I was as tiny as his four-year-old brother."

"He pulled my hair!"

Mrs. Eden looked surprised and held up a hand. "Now calm down. I'm sure Mike didn't mean it. Mike, what's going on here?"

I looked up at her and scrunched up my nose and lips. "I like that Kyle was named after her uncle. I was named after mine, and I think Eric is cute being tiny, and Tabitha's hair is really soft."

Kyle looked like she was going to be sick. "You think a boy is cute?"

"Ew," Tabitha said, scooting her chair away from me.

Eric looked like he was going to explode.

"Now, Mike," Mrs. Eden smiled, "That is all very nice to say, but we need to keep our hands to ourselves. And we need to also remember, if we don't have anything nice to say, don't say anything at all. Could you please apologise?

"I did," I said.

"So that I can hear?"

"Sorry, Kyle," I said, looking at her. "I really do like your name."

I looked back up at Mrs. Eden.

"Kyle?" Mrs. Eden asked, "do you have anything to say?"

Kyle wanted to shake her head no, but instead said, "It's okay."

"Eric," I said, "I'm sorry for calling you tiny."

"It's okay," Eric said with his arms still crossed.

167

"Sorry I pulled your hair, Tabitha. It really is soft."

Tabitha ran her hands over her pigtails and muttered, "It's okay."

Mrs. Eden ruffled my hair and walked over to her desk where she picked up her little bell and rang it. I touched my head. Grandma Boyer used to ruffle my hair, too. I suddenly felt empty like I didn't eat breakfast.

Mrs. Eden's class reminded me of the school back in Phoenix. I liked that we hardly had to sit at our desks to work, and I was allowed to sit on the floor or the rainbow rug most of the time. I'd only go back to my desk to get things, or if the teacher wanted to talk to the whole class. As the school days went by, I grew more and more comfortable with Mrs. Eden. Her days were really organised and I liked it. I knew what to do and what was expected and I thrived in that environment. Mrs. Eden never had an unkind word and seemed to have an unending patience with me. At the end of the day, she always gave me a compliment as I left. At first, I kept looking away and tried to hide my nervous smile, but as the weeks passed by, I started looking forward to hearing what she had to say to me.

"Great job today with your reading, as usual," she'd say or, "Your stories during Show and Tell were entertaining, as always."

I wished I made the other students as happy as I made Mrs. Eden, but I didn't. They didn't like my Show and Tell. They didn't like my jokes. They didn't like my compliments or my songs. I was too different to like and when I wasn't talking to Mrs. Eden, I was quietly doing my work on her rainbow rug.

"You worked so well today," Mrs. Eden said to me as I approached her at the door at the end of the day. "I'm very proud of you. Your sentences are coming along nicely. We'll be writing stories soon. I think you'll be good at writing stories. Don't you, Mike?"

I looked her in the eyes briefly and said, "Yes, Mrs. Eden. I tell good stories."

It was true. My stories always made Mrs. Eden laugh. My stories started from her having Show and Tell every Friday. I loved her reward system. Each table would get points for excellent behaviour. If someone was too disruptive or broke any of the school rules, she'd simply take points away without even saying a word. The group who'd won highest points that week could bring in something for Show and Tell. Most kids wanted to participate in it. Points were awarded individually, since most of the time we weren't together at our desks. If she saw someone working hard, she'd give them a marble so that they could drop it in the plastic bowl on one of the desks in the group. The person in the group who had the bowl was responsible for counting the points every Friday. Mrs. Eden always picked the most responsible student. I had the bowl, and this didn't seem to make the rest of the group happy. But I promised them I'd protect the points.

My first Show and Tell, I talked about Grandma Boyer and how much I missed playing games with her. Some of the students didn't seem too impressed or interested and that upset me, but I didn't say anything. I just spoke more about her to impress them. Others made sad sounds and Mrs. Eden wiped a tear or two away.

"Mike," she said, running her hand through my bangs to get them out of my eyes as Show and Tell ended when the school bell clanged together to end the day, "I hope you know you can come to me if you ever need to talk. It's hard losing a grandma. Mrs. Boyer was a very special woman. I know it can be rough having new starts all the time. This year will be different. I promise you..."

The other thing I enjoyed about Mrs. Eden's class was that I didn't go home to learn the school had called or I had a note about my disruptive behaviour. The belt on the nail fell quiet for quite some time. I liked the silence of it.

I just wished the Shadow Monster would fall silent, too.

Playing Pretend

There was always a brief moment getting off the bus after school where I almost forgot about everything that happened inside of that triangular house. I stepped off of the yellow bus and ran onto the grass that was starting to fade and towards the A-Frame. I could see through the large window in the front. Next to it was the sliding glass front door.

My brother was there smashing his face and hands against the glass. I grinned and waved. He tried to open the door, but he didn't have the strength, so I opened it, struggling myself. My sister's crib, which was Christopher's old one, was in the middle of the living room. I could see her small hands waving with excitement and she lay there looking up at the ceiling.

"Mike, guess what?" my brother said as he gave me a hug.

"What?" I said, letting him go and dropping my bag. I struggled to close the door behind me before heading over to the crib.

"She farted today," my brother said, "I heard her."

I laughed.

"Girls fart too," my brother nodded. "So does Mom."

"Mom is a girl."

My brother raised his eyebrows. "She is?"

I nodded and peered into the crib wishing I were tall enough and strong enough to reach in and lift her out.

My mom came into the room. She was walking slowly and looked pale. She smiled and gave me a hug and kiss. Christopher wanted a hug and kiss as well, so she gave them to him, too.

My mom had to take time off work and school to take care of herself as well as take care of Christina. My sister wasn't born normally, I was told. I remembered being in the hospital room before my mom was ready to give birth. We were all told that we had to leave, but my dad wouldn't leave her side. His eyes were wild. I was worried the Shadow

171

Monster was going to appear at the hospital, so I wanted to stay close to my mom too, but I couldn't. I didn't like hospitals. The last time I saw Grandma Boyer in one she looked like my mom. She was pale and weak and teary eyed.

I was told that they had to cut my mom's belly open so Christina could be born. There were so many days we could only visit her and Christina in the hospital. It was just me, Christopher and my dad at home. Christopher and I pretty much just played on our own. The only time we interacted with our dad was when we were eating and even then it was mostly Christopher asking him questions. He had no patience with us and the large sigh he gave when we were finished eating, I could tell he was glad he didn't have to deal with us until next time we ate.

So I winced as I watched my mom reached in slowly to lift my sister out of the crib and groan with pain. She had shown me where they had cut her and sometimes I helped change her bandage, but that was weeks ago. Now it was mostly just tender. I tried to stop her from bending over and picking up things by rushing to pick them up for her. I couldn't do that yet with Christina.

I went over to the couch. The soap operas were playing on TV. I grinned and wondered if my two favourite characters on General Hospital would get back together. My mom put Christina into my arms. My brother crawled up next to me on the couch and sighed softly. He loved it when I held our sister because sometimes when mom wasn't looking, I slipped her into his lap so he could have a turn of holding her, too.

I looked down at her face and grinned. I sniffed the air and it still smelt fresh. I had learnt from Christopher and more so with Christina that it was important to check her diapers. When I was around, I'd help change her and feed her. I got to do it more with Christina than I did with Christopher because I was older.

"Did you do this with me?" my brother asked.

I nodded, "Yes, I helped take care of you."

My brother leaned his head against my shoulder and sighed, "I love you."

We sat there watching General Hospital for a bit longer before my mom returned from the kitchen and said it was time to feed her.

"It's okay," I said, reaching out for the bottle. "I'll do it."

She gave me the bottle and slowly slid into the seat near us. She sighed happily, "Thank you for helping your momma."

I shrugged. I didn't mind. That was my job. I was supposed to take care of my mom and my brother and now my sister.

"When is Dad coming home?" my brother asked my mom.

My heart skipped a bit and that's when my illusion of coming home from school to a safe house disappeared. Whenever my dad was mentioned, there was always a part of my chest and stomach that panicked.

"Not till late," she said, watching the TV intently.

I was watching it intently too. I think they were about to kiss. The camera focused on the man and I grinned. He had a nice smile, but he was mischievous. He was my favourite. We got to watch TV more often now that dad was working again. He had to work while mom was recovering. I liked it better when mom was home so I could take care of her.

I looked at the wall in the living room where my dad's belt hung on its nail. I couldn't help it. I always looked at, worried it had moved or someone was going to go towards it because I did something wrong. But this time it was missing.

"Mom," I said, trembling, "where's dad's belt?"

Her eyes never left the tv screen, "He needed it for work."

I nodded slowly. I was glad it was gone. I hoped it was for good.

The mornings were safer now and so was the time after school before he came home from work. Most nights when he did get home, the rest of us had already gone to bed. In the mornings, he'd still be asleep but that didn't matter. I was off to school and would always come home to an eager brother waiting at the sliding glass door and a mom who was relieved that I was taking over. I could almost pretend things were normal.

173

My mornings were now becoming the same each day. They were just
Mrs. Eden's days. Organised. The same. There was no screaming
anymore. There wasn't things breaking or Shadow Monsters raging.

I got out of bed, fed Whiskey, gave her fresh water and then made
breakfast for my brother and me. It would always be one of our
favourites. Fruity Pebbles. Captain Crunch. Today, it was Count
Chocula. I had poured the last of it in our bowls.

My mom came in and ruffled my hair, kissed Christopher on the cheek
and wished us good morning as she made herself a pot of coffee. She
had poured the last of her coffee into the filter. She tossed the empty
bag into the bin. She noticed the empty box of cereal in it as well and
went to the cupboards opening and closing them.

"It looks like we're running out of food," she said, and went out into
the living room to feed Christina while she waited for the coffee to
brew.

I sat there and watched my brother eat. I looked down at my bowl with
a hand slowly rising to my mouth. My stomach was beginning to hurt.

"All done," my brother said and slid off the table. "Do you have to go
to school?"

I nodded as he hugged me. "Yes. I have to go. I have to help."

My brother pulled out of the hug and joined my mom in the kitchen.

I opened the fridge and saw that it was getting empty too and slid my
bowl of cereal onto a shelf. I was saving it for my brother for breakfast
the next morning.

"I pledge the allegiance to the flag ..." we all said together. My left hand was on my heart.

At first, Mrs. Eden had tried to correct it. She had taken me aside at the beginning of the school year. She had tried to explain why it was important to put my right hand over my heart during the pledge.

"The salute to the flag used to be different a long time ago," Mrs. Eden explained, "We used to hold our right hand up into the air but then came a very bad man who changed all that. He turned that salute to mean something more sinister."

"Sinister?"

"Bad," she explained further. "He killed millions of innocent people. So things changed and the hand that once was held in the air came down to cover our hearts. Covering our hearts, and taking off our hats if we wear one, shows that we are honest, and loyal to our country."

"But why the right hand? Why can't I use my left?"

Mrs. Eden paused. "Mike, I don't know."

"But you're the teacher," I said quietly, getting frustrated that no one could tell me why.

"I have a guess," she said. "But I don't like my guess."

"What's your guess?"

"Before I say," Mrs. Eden smiled, "Can you tell me one thing?"

"What?"

"Why is it so important for you to use your left hand? Why can't you use your right?"

"I was born this way," I said. "My Grandma Boyer said it makes me unique. She said a lot of people who are imaginative are left-handed.

175

She said I should be proud of who I am, and where I come from. If I'm not proud of who I am and where I come from then I should change it, but not for other people. For myself."

Mrs. Eden smiled. "Those are very good reasons. Mrs. Boyer could be quite wise and also quite stubborn. I see where you get your spirit."

"She was feisty, too," I said, my eyes getting wet. I fought to keep them dry.

Mrs. Eden sat back, "Well, my guess is that more people are right-handed. Did you know that in some schools they used to tie the left hand behind student's body to force them to use their right? Many years ago, some people believed the left hand was evil, but that is a load of poppycock."

I laughed, "I'm not evil!"

"Sometimes," she teased me, and poked me in the belly. "No, you are quite right. You're not. You're a good person. You know what, Mike? You know what I think? And this is just my opinion."

"What?" I asked, protecting my belly just in case it got poked again.

"If you want to hold your left hand up to your heart because it is you, then do it. You're left-handed. You want to say the pledge. You want it to come from your heart, so why change who you are? You remember that always," Mrs. Eden suddenly went really serious in her voice, "You remember what your grandma said. You are unique. You are you. You are a kind and sensitive boy who isn't afraid to say what he thinks and feels. And you do this from a place of love and kindness. Don't change that for the world. Not even when people try to tell you that you're wrong."

"Or that I'm evil?"

"Or that you're evil," she smiled. "Because you aren't. You're just a feisty, stubborn old lady like your grandma."

"Hey!" I exclaimed. "I'm not old!"

Friday's work ended early, and after lunch everyone would be eager to watch the clock on the wall as it ticked closer to an hour before school ended. When that hour hand struck the 2, Mrs. Eden would stop whatever it was she was doing, even if she were in the middle of a sentence, and walk towards the far corner of the room. She'd unveil a table counter from underneath a blanket, and put on a funny hat like a baseball cap but with no top to it. The visor was always a different colour each week. She'd put on her glasses. She had glasses like Grandma Boyer. They hung around her neck on a chain.

"All right, boys and girls." Mrs. Eden put on a voice like an excited saleswoman. "You know how this works. The person who is the Cup Keeper will silently count your marbles. The Cup Keeper will then pick the next person to be the Cup Keeper for next week. That person will count the marbles again, to make sure there are no mistakes."

She held up a hand and pointed a finger up in the air, "Remember. Everyone makes mistakes, and that's okay as long as we are the best that we can be."

She dropped her hand and hovered it over her counter full of prizes like she was on the Price Is Right, "After you are finished counting, each group will have a turn to come to—"

Everyone said it with her, "Mrs. Eden's Super Supermarket!"

We fell silent quickly as she continued. Our excitement was building as she deepened her voice mysteriously, "Where you can look at things that might interest you. Then you will go back to your desks and discuss what it is you'd like your table to buy. Don't forget to tell me your total when you come up to Mrs. Eden's Super Supermarket, though, because the winning table also gets to bring in something from home next week during our Show and Tell."

When she said, "Show and Tell," Mrs. Eden flung out her hands and wiggled like she was showing off a prize on a game show. We all laughed.

I started counting. Kyle and Tabitha were counting too. I could see their mouths moving, and I had to stop and recount quickly because they distracted me. Eric was up on his knees next to his chair as our number got higher and higher.

He'd turn to look at the other tables and then whisper back, "Some tables have stopped counting."

We finished at twenty-seven. I put the marbles back into our bowl.

"Don't lose your marbles!" Mrs. Eden called as she heard marbles getting dropped back into the bowl. She stood there laughing at herself.

When our marbles were back in the bowl, I grinned over at Eric, "Would you like to be the next Cup Keeper?"

Tabitha sat back in her chair with a huff. "Of course you'd pick Eric."

Kyle muttered, "If I was a boy, you'd pick me."

Eric took the bowl eagerly and started counting them over.

"You don't need to count them," Kyle said. "He's right. There's twenty-seven."

"It's my job now," Eric sniffed, and started counting again.

I called out to Mrs. Eden, who was patiently dancing behind the counter of her pretend supermarket. Some groups were already going up to look at her wares. "Why is it called a Cup Keeper when the marbles are really in a bowl?"

"Hey!" Jason called out from another table, "I just asked her that!"

Mrs. Eden laughed. "Bowl Keeper doesn't have a nice ring to it. Cup Keeper sounds better."

We all counted our marbles. Jason almost lost *his* marbles when he spilled them off the table.

"Congratulations," Mrs. Eden clapped her hands, "to all tables winning their marbles. Not one table had an empty bowl, and that's awesome. It shows just how well this class works together. And congratulations to Jason's table for finding his missing marbles."

Mrs. Eden kept giggling to herself.

"What's so funny?" Vicky asked, still traumatised over the spilled bowl. Vicky liked everything organised and neat. Jason did not. I overheard them arguing a lot at their table. They lost most of their points because of their arguing. They'd go silent when they'd see Mrs. Eden come to their desk and silently take their marbles away.

"Ten marbles to the table that figures it out first," she winked and continued, "I hope everyone liked what I had for sale and your table finds great use for your selected items. And finally, congratulations to Mike's table with twenty-seven marbles! Next week, you all will be able to bring in one item for Show and Tell."

She did the hands again and we all laughed.

Jason folded his arms, "That's not fair. Why does his table have to win?"

Mrs. Eden looked like she didn't hear him and continued, "Now, everyone return the marbles to me, please. The new Cup Keeper can come up and empty them back into my jar."

Scott, a quiet boy from the table next to mine, called out as he returned his marbles to Mrs. Eden, "Good job, Mike's table!"

Vicky emptied her bowl and returned back to the table where Jason and the rest of the group waited. They were quietly muttering to themselves.

"Thank you," I smiled back to Scott, as he returned to his seat.

Once the bowls were empty and we were sitting quietly at our desk, Mrs. Eden walked over to Scott's table. "This group will start with an extra five marbles next week for Scott's excellent manners. Winning isn't everything. Sometimes the way you lose is far more fulfilling."

Jason called out, "Yeah, good job, Mike's table!"

Mrs. Eden put a finger in the air, "Ah ah. As much as I appreciate you trying, Jason, I cannot forget how your table felt it wasn't fair. And don't think I haven't heard what your table has been whispering."

Mrs. Eden walked over to my table and stood next to Eric. She reached into the jar she was carrying and dropped a marble into our bowl. "And one extra marble to this table for Mike's magnificent manners when Scott gave his congratulations."

Eric, Tabitha and Kyle grinned at me and I pretended to bow in my seat. They giggled and when Mrs. Eden asked us to move to the rainbow rug for Show and Tell, we all did the dancing hands and sat together.

I loved Show and Tell. You got to hear about lives of the other students. Some of them had great adventures.

Tabitha talked about her older sister a lot. "So, she likes to spin her hair in her finger while she talks, and when she chews gum, my mom says she's a cow. So sometimes when she passes my brothers they moo at her and we all laugh. My sister had friends over last weekend and all they talked about was boys. My brothers turned off her bedroom light while they were in there and scared them with roars and growls. My brothers say that boys will never like them because girls have cooties. Mrs. Eden, what are cooties?"

"They're made up, and I don't want to hear about anyone having cooties in this classroom. Anyone who believes in cooties loses their marbles," Mrs. Eden threatened.

Kyle talked about baseball as she showed us her new baseball, "The ball went flying over my fence. I thought for sure I would hear glass breaking, but I didn't. My dad just stood there with his hand covering the sun from his eyes. He looked at my brother and asked him why he couldn't play sports like I do. I told Dad that sometimes girls are just better at sports."

Jason called out, "What? No way?!"

Mrs. Eden held up a finger. "Ah ah ah. We've talked about the rules. No one in the audience speaks, or their Show and Tell gets cancelled."

Jason went quiet and our eyes met. I shook my head slowly and turned my attention back to Kyle, who was already heading back to her spot next to Tabitha and Vicky.

"Mike," Mrs. Eden called, "your turn."

I gulped and stood up. Mrs. Eden's big red seat looked so comfortable and it was.

I sat on the seat and cleared my throat, "I have a grandma named Grandma Stoneburner. She loves to sing and play the tambourine. She loves to cook. She loves to watch TV. She lives in Arizona and I'm still her grandson even though we haven't seen each other in a very long time. I love her even though we had to move here, and all my hopes and dreams were lost. But one day I met another grandma named Grandma Boyer. She loved to sing and play games. She loved to win. Sometimes I'd say she was cheating, but she always said no, and that she was just using her resources. She loved to cook and have all her family come over. After she'd watched her soap operas Grandma loved to go exploring outside with me. She used to live in Beaverton, but she doesn't now. She died because she was sick and didn't tell anybody. So my Grandpa Boyer sold everything but my Aunt Shelly saved some things, and my mom has them now. They're in our A-Frame, but our cupboards are getting empty because we're running out of food. But my brother won't starve because I saved my cereal for him for tomorrow. My sister won't starve because she's just a baby and my mom feeds her. Thank you for listening."

The class clapped for me and turned to Mrs. Eden to hear who was next. Mrs. Eden was clapping too but she had a worried look on her face. I smiled at her and then returned to the rug. I whispered to Eric that he was next. Eric scooted away from me. I crinkled my mouth up a bit but turned to Mrs. Eden's seat as she called up Eric.

Starving

Saturday mornings weren't as quiet as they once had to be, but I still could not scream and shout the theme song when Thundercats came on TV, even when it was just repeats. But at least we could talk aloud, using indoor voices like we had to at school. My brother and I would spend each Saturday morning watching those cartoons while we ate breakfast. Come Saturday afternoon, both of us would be outside if the weather allowed, playing with our toys in the grass. Sometimes we'd go exploring in the woods. Being older now, I could take Christopher a little bit farther. Whiskey was much older, too, and would lead us to her favourite places.

The woods were thick with trees. Because it was fall, some of the trees would drop acorns that squirrels would quickly snatch up and take away to their secret lairs and hiding spots. If we were quiet enough, we'd be able to watch a doe with her young as they explored for food. As we walked on, rabbits would sometimes dart out from bushes, and we always heard the robins and the bluejays up high. It wouldn't take us long before we no longer saw the house and only saw the trees. If we went deep enough, we'd arrive at a neighbour's house that was closer to the paved road leading into Coleman.

But Whiskey wasn't travelling far from home lately, and one day, when my mom picked her up, we found out why. She was pregnant.

"She's going to have a kitten?" I exclaimed.

"Cats have a litter of kittens," my mom replied.

"A litter?" I asked, thinking of trash thrown on the ground.

"Yes, a litter," my mom answered. "That's what's it's called when a cat gives birth to kittens."

"She'll have more than one?!" I gasped.

As Whiskey's belly grew, she stayed closer and closer to home. She picked a spot under a tree where the grass grew the longest. The tree wasn't far to our back door. This tree was the biggest in our yard and at one point had a tire swing put on one of its thick branches. We had a big yard and with dad working nights and sleeping during the day, he

183

rarely mowed our lawn so the grass was thick. Whiskey's spot soon started looking like a nest the more she rested in it. When I wanted to find her, I no longer called out to her. I just went to that spot and picked her up to take her inside. Soon she'd start to growl at me when I tried to pick her up.

"What's wrong, Whiskey?" I said, quickly removing my hands from her belly, and that's when I understood. "Oh. I can't move you. You have babies in there."

I stared at her as she curled herself up again. "But how am I going to feed you? And you need water as well. Are you still going to walk to the backdoor or do I need to bring it to you?"

I stood up and paced back and forth and her bright green eyes followed me. The black slits in the middle were thin. They only got big when she was upset, playful, or it was dark. Her fudge-and-copper coloured fur rippled a bit and I wondered if that was the kittens moving, or the breeze as the fall continued to get closer to winter.

I walked towards the house. I had to cross the driveway, but before I reached it, I walked through the area where my brother and I were playing toys the day we had to rush over to Grandma Boyer's house. We hadn't played in that area since. It was the same day I dropped my GI Joe action figure, the one dressed as a hawk. I missed that toy, but I couldn't find it in the grass. When my dad next mowed, I searched again, but GI Joe wasn't there, nor did I ever hear the crunch from the lawnmower when my mom decided to mow it. I knew that crunch. I had lost toys before, and the blade of the lawnmower had killed them. I tried to be so careful.

When I got to the back door I looked behind me over to Whiskey's nest. It was too far away from her food bowl and water in their spot by the back steps, left out for the nights that she stayed outside. Sometimes she didn't like to be indoors. That's when I saw it. Near the shed. An old cardboard box. I had an idea. I rushed into the house and grabbed my Grandma Boyer's quilt, the one she hadn't finished. I went back outside and grabbed the big box. I put it on its side next to the food and water bowls with the quilt tucked inside.

I called to her, "Whiskey, kitty kitty kitty kitty. Here, kitty. Come here."

I heard her meow but the thick grass area didn't move. She wasn't coming. I put my fingers up into my mouth and thought about how I would get her to come. I rushed back inside.

I opened the cupboard under the sink where her food was stored, and wondered if she was running out too, like we'd run out of cereal, but I found a new bag. I opened the bag, took a handful of her food out, even though it wasn't her dinnertime yet, and walked back outside. I exited the A-Frame again and a few pellets of her food dropped on the floor.

I poured the food into the empty bowl. It clattered loudly as I said, "Whiskey, kitty kitty kitty kitty!"

The leaves and grass rustled, and Whiskey wobbled as fast as she could towards me, and more importantly, to the food. If I'd had Doritos, she would have run faster even if she were pregnant with a hundred litters of kittens.

Whiskey stuffed her face with the food. I laughed and scratched her ears, and down her back stopping before her tail, which I did not touch. She was very protective of her tail, and even more protective of her white belly, even before she was pregnant. We couldn't touch the bottom of her feet either. I think she was ticklish, but cats didn't laugh when they were tickled. They bit you, or wrapped themselves around your arm or leg and kicked at it till you promised never to tickle them again. At least, that's what Whiskey did.

When she was finished eating, she had a drink of water and then rubbed up against me a little before starting to head towards the tree.

"Oh, no," I giggled. "I have a better idea."

I gently reached under her ribs and pulled her into the box. Whiskey protested with a meow followed by a growl. She exited the box and headed towards the tree, but I put her back into the box. This time she nipped at my hand.

"Whiskey, no," I said. "This nest is better. It has our quilt and it's in a box, and it's near your food and water. I pushed the back of her spine down where the beginning of her tail started to make her sit. She complied, but stood as soon as I let go.

She looked at me with her green eyes as if to say, "I will leave this place."

"No, Whiskey, look," I said, and patted the quilt.

She sniffed at it. Her ears and long whiskers twitched. She looked at me again and then turned her butt towards me.

"Whiskey, ew," I said, curling my lip.

She then walked in circles, which made me smile. I knew what the circles meant. She was patting down the space with her paws to make it comfortable. She was always marking her territory. It would now be her new nest. I just knew it.

"See," I said, "and I feel better if you have a nest closer to home."

She lay down and rested her head on her front paws. She looked up at me for a moment, and, seeing I wasn't going to take no for an answer, she slowly closed her eyes.

And that's where Whiskey stayed when she wasn't in the mood to be in the house or go for our adventures in the woods. That's where she was Friday night and where I found her Saturday morning when I went outside to feed her. When I came back in, Mom was in the kitchen pouring us cereal.

"Mike," she said, "you didn't eat your cereal yesterday. I found it in the fridge all soggy so I made you a fresh bowl. I know you don't like it soggy."

I gasped, "That was for Christopher so he doesn't starve!"

"Starve?" my mom laughed. "Don't be silly. I got you Captain Crunch this time, though. I know it's one of your favourites."

"When did you get that?" I wondered, noticing the fridge was full again when she put the milk away.

"At the grocery store," she said, "where we buy our food."

I sat down at the table as she placed my bowl in front of me. I guess we weren't starving after all.

186

Dad woke up shortly after the cartoons ended and just before the afternoon movies or long ads about all the weird things you could buy. That's when the TV would go off, and Christopher and I would either play board games in the living room, toys, or go outside. Mostly, we went outside.

My brother and I checked on Whiskey, but the moment we neared the box, she hissed.

"She's in one of her moods," I warned Christopher. "We better not bother her."

"What's wrong with Whiskey?"

I shrugged as I watched her pant at us. "Maybe she's thirsty. Her bowl is there. She'll get it. Let's go play."

We didn't play long when a car pulled up into the dirt driveway. We stood up and ran towards the back door where we knew all cars eventually parked. As the car grew closer, I saw Mrs. Eden waving from the window.

My eyes almost popped out of my head as I screamed into the house, "MOM! MRS. EDEN IS HERE!"

I heard a gruff voice inside, "Why don't people call before they come over? It better not be your sister again. I've told her…"

My mom opened the back door and asked, "Who is it?"

I pointed to the car, where Mrs. Eden was opening up the backseat and pulling out some supermarket bags. "It's my teacher. Mrs. Eden."

My mom's eyes almost popped out of her head, too. "What is she doing here?"

She took the three steps that led to our driveway and walked over to the car. I followed. My brother was peeking into Whiskey's box. My dad came out as well, giving me a look of warning. I was sure he thought I was in trouble. He was still in his comfy shorts with no shirt. His chest hair was like our grass. It needed to be mowed.

"Hello!" Mrs. Eden called as she struggled to carry the two large paper bags towards my mom. "Sorry to bother you on the weekend, but I felt it necessary to bring some things."

My mom adjusted her glasses. "Bring some things?"

"Yes," Mrs. Eden smiled. "Mike was telling the class you all are struggling with groceries at the moment, so the school has put together a few things. Just to get you back on your feet."

My dad snapped his head towards me and hissed, "What did you do?"

He took a step towards me. His nose was bellowing with the smoke from his cigarette. His eyes were bloodshot.

My mom looked confused and didn't know who to approach, Mrs. Eden or my dad.

Mrs. Eden called out, "Mr. Stoneburner! There's no need to be embarrassed. Mike didn't know I was coming."

My dad blinked and looked at her as if he was only just remembering she was there. He just took a puff of his cigarette and blew it up into the air. "Mrs. Eden, I'm afraid Mike lied to you."

I went wide-eyed, and my heart leapt into my throat. I wasn't a liar.

"No!" I exclaimed.

"Mike," my mom sighed, "oh my god this is embarrassing. Mike, why did you tell Mrs. Eden we had no more food?"

"You said so!" I exclaimed, avoiding my dad's angry gaze.

"I did not," my mom started, and then turned to my dad. "Oh, Dean, he must have misunderstood me. I did say we were running out of food. That's why he saved his cereal for Christopher."

Mrs. Eden just stood there with a red face. She didn't say a word. She just held the bags in her arms and watched my mother and father.

"I guess my son needs to learn to mind his own business," my dad tried to laugh, and walked with my mom towards Mrs. Eden. "We are so sorry. This is quite embarrassing."

Mrs. Eden looked over at me, "Mistakes happen. Mike does love to tell his stories. Never you mind. Take the bags anyway. I know things have been hard with your mother passing and just having a baby. Mr. Stoneburner has his new job and everything."

"You know all that?" my dad said.

Mrs. Eden smiled sweetly, batting her eyes at my dad. "You have a lovely boy who only wants what is best for his family. You must be proud to have a son who looks after his brother and sister as much as he does. How is your new baby girl anyway?"

My mom helped Mrs. Eden bring the bags into the house before they came back out again. Mrs. Eden shook Mom's hand. "Please feel free to drop in to the classroom at any time. I know it must be hard to schedule things. I'll be sending home a letter each week, just to let you both know how he's doing. I'm sorry for intruding on your weekend. I'm sure family time is important to you all. I'll see you at school Monday morning, Mike."

She waved at me and got into her car and my mom talked with her through the window. Mrs. Eden would look over her shoulder at my dad and then smile over at me and wink.

"By the way, congratulations to Whiskey on her new litter of kittens!"

She drove away and left us all in silence.

After Mrs. Eden had left, we turned around to see Christopher cradling a wet kitten. Whiskey was at the opening of the box, where I had left it, cleaning up the ones underneath her as well as howling up at the one Christopher held. Whiskey was a mother.

After her visit, Mrs. Eden sent home a letter with me at the end of each week. A few of the other children, like Jason, Tabitha, and a couple of other boys, would get a letter too. I asked Mrs. Eden why I was getting a letter now and she just told me that it was so my dad knew how well I was doing in school.

My mom would read the letter, which was always addressed to my dad and not her. Mom would hug me and tell me that Dad was going to love to read the letter when he woke up Saturday afternoon. Dad's hours changed to the night shift again at a machine shop, working on car parts. I remembered when he worked on airplane parts in Arizona. I overheard him tell my mom that he preferred the night shift anyway. I didn't like it. The moment he changed back to it we had to be quiet again during the day while he slept. It was getting harder and harder to pretend that everything was okay.

I wanted to move Whiskey together with her babies into the house, but I had two people against the idea. First, Whiskey didn't want to move from the box and she stayed very close to the kittens. She wouldn't let anyone near them except for me. So it was my job to make sure they were safe. Second, my dad didn't want a bunch of cats inside the house.

"Besides, they're loud. I can hear them outside while I'm sleeping. Imagine how loud they'd be if they're inside," I heard him grumble one afternoon after he'd woken up.

I never argued with him about anything. Arguing made him angry and sometimes my mom would tell me that if she didn't argue so much with him while he was drinking, he wouldn't get so angry. It was better when he got his way.

The mornings were silent again. When I was getting up to go to school, my dad had just gotten home. The sound of his fan filled the living room from upstairs. I missed the mornings we'd talk to each other or play music or watch tv. But that was only because he had left for work already. My mornings also had an extra chore. I made sure

190

Christopher was taken care of but I would also open the back door and look over at the box to check Whiskey and the kittens.

I missed Whiskey sleeping in bed with me and I wasn't sleeping well. I yawned and opened up the back door. It was starting to get cold. My mom promised the kittens would be indoors during the winter, even though I heard my dad at night argue with her. I'd silently send her my thoughts, hoping I'd be like Jean Gray and send her telepathic powers. I'd tell her to stop arguing so the Shadow Monster didn't come again.

As I stepped out onto the cement stairs leading down to the driveway to the cars, I could tell something was not right. The box had moved, and it was empty.

I scrambled down the steps and went over to the box. "Whiskey? Whiskey? Kitty kitty kitty?"

There was no sound. She didn't answer back. I pulled the quilt out. It was dusty and smelled like cats, but there were no cats inside of it. The food bowl was empty because I hadn't fed her yet. The water bowl was tipped over. My heart was pounding. Tears were building up behind my nose and up into my eyes. I couldn't swallow, and calling for her was getting tough.

That's when I heard her. "*Reawr.*"

My head twitched to the sound and I turned my left ear towards where I thought it had come from, but I didn't wait to hear it again. If I was a Thundercat, I would have been Cheetara right at that moment. She could run really fast. I bounded over towards the big tree in the yard with the tall grass. I fell onto my knees and saw her instantly. Whiskey had nestled herself into the long grass, huddled against the roots of the tree that protruded from the dirt, with her kittens. Except, they weren't all there. There had been eight kittens. Now I counted only five.

"Whiskey," I cried, "where are the rest of your kittens?"

She gave me a sad little meow and was desperately cleaning her kittens with her tongue. They were feeding off her like Christina did with my mom unless my mom was too sore and had to use a bottle. I didn't want to disturb them, so I ran back to the house.

"Mom!" I cried, pushing the door open, "Whiskey's kittens are gone!"

She came out into the kitchen holding Christina in her arms. She had been feeding her. My brother was right behind. He was still waking up and looked cranky.

"What do you mean they're gone?" she asked.

"Whiskey had eight kittens, but there's only five now!"

My mom followed me outside and when she saw the box she gasped, "Where are they?"

"Whiskey has them in her first nest," I said, pointing to the tree.

"Cats don't have nests," but she still followed me over and I pushed aside the grass to reveal Whiskey's hiding place. Whiskey hissed at us and I let go of the grass. "There's only five."

My mom nodded and motioned for me to follow her back to the house. "Well, fix up the box and her food and water and I'll figure this out. Don't want you to miss the bus so hurry."

I did what I was told, but I didn't want to go to school after I was done. I wanted to stay with Whiskey. I wanted to find the other three kittens, but no matter how hard I fought and cried, I was on that annoying yellow bus heading to Mrs. Eden's class.

When I got back home in the afternoon, I ignored my brother at the sliding door and went along the side to the back door. The box only had my quilt. The food and water bowls were untouched, and, as I headed towards the tree, I could see Whiskey standing near the tall grass. Her kittens were wandering around. There were still five of them. I walked up to her and gave her a scratch around the ears and chin. I smiled and went to the back door where my mom was waiting with the door open. Christopher was making his way down the steps but stopped when he saw me coming.

"Mom," I asked, "why aren't they in the house?"

"Well," my mom sighed, "you're the closest we've gotten to her today, and your father still doesn't want a bunch of kittens running around inside. It's still warm enough outside. They'll be fine. I think the other ones just got sick and Whiskey had to take care of them. It's what animals do."

"Oh, that's horrible. Can't we take them to a hospital?"

My mom shook her head, "You need to trust Whiskey. She will take care of them."

I looked out the back door towards Whiskey and felt sorry for her and her sick kittens. I closed the door.

That night in bed I woke up to a loud scream. I sat up in bed and stared at the door. There was no light pouring in from the cracks of the door. I waited to hear the thuds and my mom to scream again, but it didn't come. The thuds didn't, anyway.

The scream had come from outside.

"*Reeeooowwrrrr,*" the scream wailed, and my stomach jumped into my throat at its sound.

It was Whiskey. She was screaming. I recognised her voice. I sat up in bed, but I knew I couldn't leave. I would get in trouble and my dad had the night off. He had a couple of nights off of work. He referred to those days as his weekend, even though those days happened during the week.

Soon the night fell back into silence and I cried myself to sleep. I wanted to get out of bed. I wanted to go check on her but my legs wouldn't move. It was just like when I saw the shadows of my mom and dad but I just couldn't go down the stairs to save her.

"Oh, Mike," she sighed. "It was an owl. An owl got her kittens."

We all sat in silence as we ate breakfast. My dad just smoked his cigarette and blew it out of his nose. His eyes squinted at me. Usually we didn't eat breakfast when dad was up, but mom insisted. I wished I was back in bed with Whiskey. I didn't want to eat either.

Mom moved Whiskey's food and water bowls inside. Even when we poured out her food, she didn't leave my bedroom where my mom had put her. I was so glad she was okay. When I tried to pick her up off the bed she just sadly protested, and I left her. I kissed the top of her head and rubbed my face along her chin and into her neck. She returned the cuddles.

"I'm going to school, Whiskey, but I'll be back. No owl will get me."

For the next few nights, I dreamt the same thing. I'd wake up in a sweat and hold Whiskey close. Sometimes if it was so bad and I heard that my mom was out in the kitchen I'd wander out in tears. She'd just take me back to bed and tell me it was just a dream.

I dreamt that I slid off my bed and ran to my bedroom door. I opened the door, and the darkness of the bathroom across the way scared me. I dreamt of Whiskey's scream echoed throughout the kitchen. I ran out into the room and turned to my right to the back door. I unlocked the handle and tried to open it, but there was a chain up at the top that stopped it from opening. I ran to the dining-room table and dragged a chair to the door. I had done this before when Grandma Boyer had come over one day but Mom and Dad weren't home. She wasn't happy to learn my brother and I were on our own, and she stayed with us until my parents had come back.

I stood on the chair and unlatched the chain. I pushed the chair aside and switched on the outside light. I looked out the door.

The light didn't reach all the way past the tree. The tree was just on the edge. I could see a dark shape running around the bottom of the tree. The scream was coming from there and I knew that shape was her. I ran across the driveway and into the grass, which was slippery with dew. The shape stopped running but it didn't stop screaming.

Whiskey looked at me. Her eyes reflected the outside light. Her fur was puffed out. She was terrified. She was angry. She was searching the grass. I got down on my knees and looked for her kittens, but they were all gone.

"Kitties?!" I screamed out.

I heard the rustle of branches and when I looked up a dark shape flew down at me.

Whiskey leapt into the air with her own scream and the shape darted away. I could hear the kittens from above us, and then I never heard from them again. Whiskey was running madly around the tree. I wanted to go inside. Tears were streaming down my face. I was so scared. The Shadow Monster knew how to fly, and I wanted to go hide. But Whiskey needed me. Whiskey needed me to help her find her kittens and I wouldn't stop until she stopped.

After a while, Whiskey stopped running. She slowly sniffed the air and the long grass. I fell backwards on my backside. She looked over at me. Her whiskers were wiggling. Her eyes glowing as she approached me. She jumped into my lap and mewed. Her small nose blew warm air against my face. A rustling in the trees terrified us both. She hissed. I yelped. She jumped off my lap and nipped at my leg. I got up and we both ran towards the backdoor. We could hear the noises in the branches and I could hear the swoop of the Shadow Monster as I imagined it flying towards me. His long claws would reach out to my back. I could imagine the pain I would feel if he caught me. I scooped up Whiskey awkwardly. She growled and howled as both of us went up the steps and I closed the door behind us.

Our nightmare was over.

195

As I sat on the annoying, yellow bus watching my house slowly disappear from my window, I felt sad and sick. I wanted to stay with Whiskey and make sure she was okay. I knew how she felt losing the ones you loved. I lost my Grandma and Grandpa Stoneburner when we left Phoenix. I lost my rocking horse in the house fire. I lost my dad to the Shadow Monster. I lost my Grandma Boyer and all the other family who stopped spending time with us.

Whiskey had kittens. I would have helped raise her babies, but my mom insisted the Owl got them. I didn't even know what an owl looked like, I don't think. I'd ask Mrs. Eden.

"Hey, runt," a voice called out from the seat behind me.

I lifted up my head against the back of the seat and saw one of the big kids looking over at me. I turned my head around.

She sniffed and glared at me. "You shouldn't be sitting back here so far."

I took a deep breath. I wasn't in the mood to deal with the big kids. There weren't any seats right in front, or anyone who was willing to share their seat. This seat was empty, but on the borderline of the rear of the bus, where the big kids sat.

"There were no seats," I said, and turned back towards the window. I imagined Whiskey on my bed singing her sad meows. I imagined them to be her tears as she curled up with the unfinished quilt. I imagined her thinking of that owl and also thinking of me alone on an annoying, yellow bus dealing with an annoying, big kid who was kicking the back of my seat.

A tear slowly sunk down my face until I could taste it on my lips. I parted them and began to sing softly.

Whenever I was sad back in Phoenix, my Grandma Stoneburner would rock me on her wooden rocking chair like she did when I was a baby. "Hush little baby don't say a word …"

Whenever I was sad, my mom would hold me in her arms and wipe away my tears, "I'm gonna shout, Hallelujah, my savior is always on my side …"

Whenever I was sad, and I stayed over at Grandma Boyer's house, she'd make sure she beat me at a few games first, and if that didn't work, she'd hold me in her arms, "I found a peanut, found a peanut, found a peanut just now …"

Whenever I was sad at home, Whiskey would appear and we'd curl up together in bed and I'd whisper to her, "It's beginning to rain, rain, rain, hear the voice of the Father, saying whosoever will come drink of His water …"

But Grandma Stoneburner was far away. My mom was always the one who was sad now, and I had to hold her and sing to her. And Grandma Boyer wasn't around anymore because she had to leave me. Whiskey was the only one remaining, and I'd left her alone with no one to look after her. If I had gone outside like I wanted to, I might have saved them.

I closed my eyes allowing the tears to fall and wet my dry lips. I whispered the song I always sang with Whiskey. I was going to sing it to myself. I had no one else. I'd have to take care of me. I imagined the bus stopping. A little boy got on. It was me. I'd be surprised, but he'd ask to sit with me and I'd say yes because I knew what it felt like when people said no. He'd sit next to me and he'd hug me. He'd tell me everything was going to be okay. He'd sing to me. He'd sing away my tears. So, that's what I did. I sang.

The big kid behind me swore, saying the word my parents said if they dropped something, and then said, "I think the little runt is singing."

I closed my eyes tighter and sang a bit louder. I didn't want to hear her and I just wanted to ignore my seat being kicked over and over. I could feel it was her knees or feet or her hands. I felt two lumps just pushing into my back through the seats.

I felt something brush against my hair and I winced. Sometimes when I said something my dad wouldn't think was "smart", he'd hit me across the back of the head. I imagined that was what she was trying to do to me. I missed Emily and her brother Eric, not the Eric from my class he was too small to stand up for me, but big Eric, who drove now, would have told them to stop. He used to.

She swore again and she must have been leaning forward in her seat because I heard her above my head, "Hey, runt, you have a huge booger in your hair. That's so gross. Don't you wash your hair? Hey, guys, this kid wiped a booger in his hair!"

My eyes snapped open. I did have a bad habit of picking my nose, but I was sure that it wasn't me this time. My hands were nowhere near my head. I stiffened, remembering I felt something brush against it earlier, and slowly raised my hand to the back of my head. I patted my hair slowly, but couldn't feel anything.

"Oh, gross!" she hollered. "He's spreading his booger through his hair! You're sick, runt!"

I just wanted her to go away. Didn't she know I was having a bad day? Someone needed to tell her.

"Stop it," I whined back at her. "I don't have a booger in my hair."

"It's so gross," she hollered with a hint of a laugh. "You totally do, man. It's all over the back of your head. You should wash your hair. Don't you wash your own hair?"

I don't know why, but I closed my eyes and thought of Grandma Boyer. I imagined the bus stopping and it was actually Grandma Boyer driving the bus. She got up off her seat and walked down the aisle towards me. She was chewing gum like the bus driver did and it made me laugh a little. I squeezed my eyes tighter and imagined her adjusting her big glasses and fluffing her large hair. She had the bus driver's wild hair and not the short curly hair. She whipped out a bar of soap. I turned around and watched her stare at the big kid and aim the soap towards her mouth.

I opened my eyes. I could still hear the girl behind me continue to tease me. I wish Grandma Boyer had been really there. I wish someone would stop the girl from teasing me. But no one did. So I started to sob.

It was silent behind me at first, but then I heard the laughter of the big kids.

"He eats his boogers, I'm telling you. The kid must be starving!"

Big kids are such jerks, I thought to myself. When I turned into a big kid, I promised to always look out for the little ones.

Out of the Ashes

Winter hit hard. The rain turned to sleet and then to ice. I hated being in the car or the bus when it slid. Luckily these big trucks went around and put salt on the main roads. Our problem was the dirt road would have to get ploughed privately by one of the neighbours.

Whiskey refused to leave the house at first, but as winter went on, she started to follow me outside. She followed me around the yard, except when I went near the trees or into snow that was too deep. She'd meow if I went too far and if she lost sight of me she panicked. I'd reappear, and she'd do quick little meows and rush up to me. Her mouth would be drooling, and she'd rub up against me or demand that I pick her up. The cold didn't allow us to stay outside for too long anyway and she'd be happiest curled up next to me inside where it was warm.

My nightmares continued through winter but it started to change. It wasn't about owls anymore. I dreamt that I jumped out of the bed but instead of landing on my old bedroom floor I landed in the grass outside. The tree stood before me. It was dark until the outside light turned on. I turned to look at it, but I was deep in the woods now. I could see the house between the trees in the distance. Whiskey was still screaming. I could see the outside light shining across the yard. I ran through the trees towards the house. I heard dogs barking behind me. I turned to look behind me. It wasn't dogs but large kittens. There were eight of them and they were barking and snarling. I tried to run faster, but I was running in slow motion. I could not get back to the house.

"Reeeoowwrr!" I heard Whiskey scream and I ran as fast as I could. "Miiiikke!"

201

The barks and snarls were right behind me now, and I felt a sharp pain in my back as they caught up to me. I'd wake up with a stabbing pain in my back.

One night, I wandered out into the living room hoping to find my mom. Whiskey had stayed in the bed. Christopher was snoring softly. I walked around the opening from the kitchen into the living room and whined.

"Mom, I had a nightmare again."

But I didn't find my mom. I found my dad. He was sitting in his chair. His right hand around his drink as he lifted it up to his mouth. I didn't know he had the night off. I heard the fan going on upstairs. I went to go back to bed, but I heard the can he was holding tap onto the TV tray he had in front of him.

"Come here, son," he growled.

I took a few steps towards him. He reached over to the couch that was beside his chair and patted the cushion. "Sit here. Watch TV with me."

I got onto the couch and my eyes widened at the screen. It was full of naked people.

"Do you know what those are? Or that is?" he grumbled and spent the rest of the video explaining and showing me things that men could do.

Things at school began to unravel. I didn't want to be touched. I wanted my own space and my patience for the other boys seemed to be gone. Eric began to bug me more and more. Instead of trusting Mrs. Eden to handle it, I'd snap back at the boys like I used to in First Grade and Kindergarten.

"Mike," Mrs. Eden said to me after I yelled at Eric, "I'm surprised at you."

Our table wasn't winning as much at table points and there were even weeks where we couldn't afford any of her prizes. Eric began to blame me more and more. During a cold, wintery recess, we were forced to stay indoors. Eric and I exploded and pushed each other.

We both were taken to the office for fighting, but only Eric's family came and got him. I had to wait in the office until the end of the day where Mrs. Eden found me and waited with me. She didn't seem to be happy and I tried to apologise.

Mrs. Eden and I took a step out of the office as the front of the school's doors slammed open and my dad stormed in. When he saw me, he gave a big breath out and in before walking quickly towards us. He was in his comfy shorts still and his buttoned up plaid shirt. He had on shoes but no socks. He definitely came straight from bed.

"Sorry!" I said quickly, and Mrs. Eden squeezed my shoulder.

"There's no need to be sorry," Mrs. Eden sounded like she was talking to my dad more than she was to me as my dad stood in front of us.

"What happened?" he growled, his eyes wild.

"We've just had a rough day. Mike has been struggling this year with his Grandma Boyer's passing as well as what has happened with Whiskey's kittens. I would be struggling, too, if I were him. We just had an incident where a boy in class was giving him a hard time. I can assure you the boy has been dealt with."

"Who was he?" my dad snarled, looking down at me.

"Eric," I quickly said, avoiding my dad's gaze.

"I want to talk to his parents. Did he touch my son? This shouldn't be happening. I shouldn't be called up in the middle of the afternoon. I work the night shift. I have to stay awake all night while everyone else gets to sleep. I have to sleep through the day, do you understand, Mrs. Eden? This should not be happening to me."

Mrs. Eden took a deep breath and replied, "I am sure you can understand how hard it would be for a young boy to deal with the loss of not only his grandmother, but a litter of kittens from his own pet. On top of that, getting into a fight at school can be quite traumatising as well. I am very thankful that he has a parent who will sacrifice his sleep to ensure that his own son is safe. That is very noble of you."

My dad paused and stared down Mrs. Eden, who did not blink once. "I want the name and number of Eric's parents. I want to speak with them."

Mrs. Eden suggested, "I feel that Mike should go home with you and get a good night's sleep."

Mrs. Eden leaned down and hugged me. "You stay strong. And don't worry about the events in the classroom. Everyone understands how hard it has been for you."

"Sorry," I said again.

Mrs. Eden held me close. "Thank you for apologising, and I need you to promise me you will never do anything like that again. If someone hurts you, you don't hurt them back. You don't throw things or break things when you get angry or frustrated. You are a talented writer. You need to use your talent with words, and talk things out."

I nodded, and was pulled away by my dad. Mrs. Eden smiled until I reached the door and then I could see the smile start to fade. She leaned against the doorframe of the office, and said something to the office lady, who was also watching us leave. I wished I knew what they were saying.

Later, my dad made me tell him what Eric's full name was. I remembered it and he spent some time looking them up in the phone book. We called a few people that had the same name until we found the right one. I was tired of talking to strangers, but he kept making me ask for Eric. He handed the phone to me after dialling another number.

My dad told me what to say: "Hello, this is Mike from Mrs. Eden's class. Is Eric there, please? It's Mike here."

I repeated it.

The woman on the other end said, "Yes. Just a minute," and I heard her say in the background, "Eric it's a friend from your class. His name is Mike."

I heard Eric say, "He's not my friend," but he answered the phone anyway.

"Hi, Eric," I said quietly, and blushed as if he could see me.

My dad said: 'You really upset me when you pushed me today. I don't like to be pushed."

I repeated it.

"Is that your dad I hear?" Eric asked.

My dad kept speaking: "We shouldn't be mean to each other. We should be friends. Eric, will you be my friend?"

I repeated my dad's words. I said it all a bit wrong, and he repeated himself. I said it again, and this time I made sure I said it correctly.

Eric stammered, "Ummm, okay. Is your dad going to talk to me?"

I heard the woman's voice in the background, "Eric, what's going on?"

I was feeling my stomach turn and just wanted the conversation to end.

"Ask him again if he will be friends," my dad said. "And I want to hear his reply."

I asked him again, "Eric, do you want to be friends?"

I held out the phone so that my dad and I could hear what Eric said.

Eric said, "Yes, we can be friends."

My dad nodded his head and walked away satisfied. "Tell him thank you and you're sorry for anything you did, and then hang up."

I sighed, "Sorry, Eric, for pushing you and calling you tiny."

The woman on the other end was closer. "Eric, is this the boy you pushed today? You better say you're sorry."

"I'm sorry for pushing you and calling you a liar," Eric muttered.

I think we both hung up the phone at the same time. I at least hoped we did.

That night as I was heading to bed, I walked around the house calling Whiskey's name. My dad hadn't gone back to sleep in the afternoon, and we had to avoid him as he sat in his chair in the living room. It was a lounge chair that had survived the fire. It matched the couch. It had wooden arms and legs, and cushions that featured scenes from the Old West. No one sat in that chair except for him. Sometimes my mom did but only when he wasn't home.

"Whiskey's outside," my dad said, as I passed by him to go upstairs to Christina's room. I wanted to see if Whiskey had jumped into the crib.

I looked at him with terror. "Outside?"

"She won't be sleeping with you, tonight," my dad growled, "You shouldn't have pushed that boy and thrown things in class."

I put my fingers up to my mouth and stepped away from him. "Okay."

I turned and went through the kitchen into my room. I jumped into my bed and cried into the pillow. My face felt like it was on fire. My whole body was shaking. What my dad said made no sense, but I still agreed with him. I shouldn't have hurt someone back. I shouldn't have thrown things around the room. My dad was right.

But then why did he do those things?

"I thought I was brave and strong," I read to the class, "my mom left me standing in the bath. I was naked and cold. The towel was resting on the counter. The bath had a sliding door that was open. She told me she'd be right back, but I was a big boy now. She had told me that. She didn't come back for a million, bazillion years. So I tried to lift my leg over the bath tub. My other foot slipped and --"

"BAM!" I shouted, clapping my hands together, making the whole class jump, even Mrs. Eden. "I hit my chin on the metal railing of the

206

bath tub door. Luckily I didn't fall through the glass door my mom left open, but my chin split open on the rail. Blood was pouring everywhere. I was screaming. I was crying. I bet if my mom looked into my chin, she would have seen my brains."

"*Eeww*," some of the class said.

I held up the photos we had gotten in a photo booth. There were five in a row. One was of me by myself. Another was underneath it with my mom and me. The others were a mixture of both.

"These are pictures of me with a huge pad over my chin to hide the stitches," I said.

The class said another, "*Eeewww!*"

Then Mrs. Eden applauded, and the class followed. "Mike, that was a very exciting story. Don't throw that away! You should keep that one."

I nodded and took my place on the rainbow rug. I was the last one to do Show and Tell today. Our table had won. We had been able to bring in something to show. I had picked the pictures and read my story. Scott had brought in a yo-yo. He was sitting at our table after Mrs. Eden had told him to swap places with Eric. Tabitha brought in a doll. Kyle brought in another baseball, but some player signed this one. I already forgot who it was.

Mrs. Eden asked everyone to pack away their things and get their bags. The sun was out. It had been a while since we had seen the sun. The light snow that spread across the ground was now melted.

"All right," Mrs. Eden said, clapping her hands. "If you guys line up at the door very quietly and walk through the halls without a sound, we might be able to sneak outside before the final bell rings so you can play before you go home. I want you to stay on the hard surfaces only. Absolutely no running. It's slippery out there."

"Yes, Mrs. Eden," we replied.

"Have a wonderful Christmas Holiday. Stay safe. And I'll see you next year!" she exclaimed as we stood silently in a line in front of her. She opened the classroom door and tiptoed out into the hallway. We followed, trying not to giggle too loudly as we copied her. The office lady waved to us as we tiptoed passed and we almost said goodbye, but

Mrs. Eden put a finger to her lips and hissed at us to stay quiet. As soon as we were out the side doors we all fell into a fit of giggles and then spread out to find a spot to play.

That's when I made my first mistake. I ran. I ran across the hard surface towards the rocky area where the twirly-slide lay waiting. It hadn't been used in days. We weren't allowed to use the play equipment most of winter.

My second mistake was, in my excitement, not to hear Mrs. Eden calling out to me. I clambered up the stairs leading to the top of the slide. It twisted in two big loops and twirled around so fast that anyone who slid down it would become dizzy when they landed on the bottom.

I squealed as I grabbed onto the bar that went across the top and swung out to land on the slide and zoom down to the bottom, and this is where I made my third and final mistake. I didn't realise how much the melting snow would make me go faster on the slide. I twirled around once but on the second twirl I flew out over the edge of the slide. My body twisted in the air and I felt my head hit something hard before the sun disappeared and I was in darkness.

I don't remember getting up, but I remember walking next to Mrs. Eden towards the school. I don't remember going into the school, but I remember sitting in the office. I don't remember my parents coming, but I remember being in the car. I don't even remember the drive home, but I remember finding myself in bed with Whiskey curled up tightly against my neck, licking the back of my ear.

We were sitting in the front yard quite far from the house. Christmas had come and gone. We were in the new year, enjoying another snowfall. Christopher and I had spent the day building snowmen around our snow fort. They were like our soldiers. The snow was so deep we were able to make walls in the fort with little windows looking out around us. We had a walkway down into our little alcove. We pretended we were at war with the neighbours, the house where Emily and Eric lived and the house to the right of them. Snowballs were our bullets for the imaginary enemies that tried to sneak into our yard.

We were just about to go inside the house to get dry and warm when a shadow passed by one of our fort windows. We looked at each with fear and excitement.

"Quick," I whispered to Christopher, "get the snowballs ready."

"Yes, sir," he said.

I had taught him to say that for our war game.

Christopher headed towards the entrance where piles of snowballs were waiting. Then the shadow appeared at the door. Christopher took a step back and then turned to run to me.

"Monster," he whimpered, holding me close. I bent down to peek out and a huge dog was blocking the way. It was the neighbour's dog. It was always inside of a fence and collared. I could see that his collar and chain were broken. The dog looked like one from TV, but this dog wasn't named Lassie. This dog was named Cassie and my dad hated her because she always barked when he was trying to sleep.

"Cassie," I said softly, holding up a hand. "Go home, Cassie."

Cassie lifted her long snout and showed her sharp teeth.

"Cassie," I urged, "Go home!"

I reached down to move my brother behind me, but he wasn't there. I turned around and saw his little legs wiggling out the other window towards the house.

I looked back at Cassie, who was now growling at me at the entrance. I didn't want her to see Christopher, so I stepped forward to make a barrier. The dog lowered herself closer to the ground. Her tail was between her legs. She glared at me with her sharp, wet teeth.

Whiskey appeared through one of our fort windows and then the fort filled with snow as everything went white around me. Whiskey had leapt towards Cassie with a howl showing her little sharp teeth and her front paws exposing her claws. The fort had collapsed. I burst through the snow and saw my brother already halfway to the house. His little legs could run fast, I had to give him that.

I turned and saw Cassie rolling around in the snow howling. I jumped away and ran a bit before turning around. She was yelping and running back towards her house across the street next to the house where Emily and Eric lived.

I saw Whiskey chasing Cassie all the way back to her yard. I could hear Cassie yelping all the way towards her cage, which was wide open. She disappeared into the back where I knew her doghouse stood in the snow.

Whiskey turned around and started walking back towards me but she didn't even stop when she neared. Her nose was up in the air as her paws daintily walked through the snow. She walked straight up to the sliding door where Christopher was waiting. My mom was standing there with it opened laughing until she snorted. I followed Whiskey, who led me straight back into the house. She didn't stop to wait for me to take my snowshoes and suit off. She went straight into the kitchen where we eventually heard her meow. We all went to see what she was up to, and laughed.

Whiskey was sitting like a regal queen next to her empty food bowl and meowed at all of us.

"I believe her majesty wants a reward for saving you," my mom said.

I laughed and bowed, "Yes, your majesty."

Christopher was already waist deep in one of the bottom cupboards where he pulled out a bag of Doritos. As soon as Whiskey saw the bag she meowed loudly with happiness, and began trotting around our legs rubbing herself against us.

Winter just kept getting worse. I was already tired of it, especially at school. Most days we weren't allowed to go outside because it was too cold or too wet. And when we did go outside, it wasn't a safe place to play. Whistles would blow from teachers who would yell out for students not to run along the payment. They'd also blast their whistles if snowball fights got too rough.

I pretty much wandered around singing songs to myself. I tried playing with the other kids but they weren't interested. My favourite part of playtime during winter was when the bell rang and we all had to go inside.

I looked forward to winter ending and spring beginning. I was pretending the flowers were fighting the snow when the bell rang. I was surprised we were allowed out. The ground was covered in icy and sloppy snow. It was perfect for snowmen, snowballs and snow forts, but everyone's snowsuits were damp by the time the bell rang.

I made my way towards the double door that led back into the hallways back to the classrooms. The snow was blurring around me. I hugged myself. I could hear kids around me taunting each other on the way back to the school building.

"Hey, Mikey!" I heard a voice call out to me from behind.

I went to turn around when something hard and sharp struck the back of my head. My eyes blurred with the snow and I blinked. My eyes went dark. I blinked again. The brightness of the snow returned as I found myself in the snow on all fours, blood dripping down my cheeks. I looked up to see a teacher heading towards me with a couple of students. I couldn't see which teacher it was who was on duty. I blinked. I was suddenly being carried but I couldn't remember being picked up. My head couldn't stay up. It kept rolling around in the teacher's arms. I blinked. I felt like I was stuck on the twirly slide. I blinked again. I was in the nurse's office. I don't believe I had been there before but the nurse flashed a bright light flash in my eyes. I was having a hard time keeping my eyes open.

"And how did you hit your head this time?" she asked me.

211

I let my eyes close.

When I woke up, I was in a vehicle. We were driving fast. The scenery flashed passed me too quickly and I had to shut my eyes to stop the spinning.

I was in a room, laying on a table with another person shining a flashlight into my eyes.

"I need you to stay awake for me, Mike," I heard a man's voice say.

I tried to keep my eyes open as best as I could. He kept talking to me. My mom kept talking to me. I tried to ask her how she got there but words weren't forming right.

"So, what I understand ..." the doctor said, touching the back of my head. It felt like that hard, sharp object was hitting me again when he touched it lightly. I cried out. "Sorry, Mike. He has a concussion, and yes, he will need a few stitches. I'm guessing a child threw a snowball at him but there was ice in it. You won't believe how many kids we get in here."

I tried to tell them that that's what happened. I tried to tell them that someone called my name. Someone threw it at me, but I still couldn't talk and to be honest, I didn't want to anymore. The more I tried to talk the sicker I felt. Besides, if I got anyone at school in trouble, they'd hate me even more.

When I was finally able to go back to school, it felt like I had been away for a whole year. I lost track of how many days I was away. I was too busy at home taking care of my brother and sister. At first, I had to stay active. I would only sleep at night with everyone else and my mom would wake me in the night to check if I was okay. Sometimes even Whiskey woke me up and we'd both go outside so she could use the toilet. I think she did that on purpose because she was worried too. My head hurt for a while, but when it finally felt better my mom started talking about going back to school. I wanted to return to school. I missed Mrs. Eden and the longer I was staying at home, the more my dad complained about it.

The morning I went back to school, before I left the house, I went and looked at my sister sleeping in the crib. She looked so peaceful.

"I want to play with you," I said quietly so as not to wake her. "Dolls are like action figures, just bigger. I want you to play snow forts and have snowball fights. Why can't we do whatever we want?"

I sighed and walked the length of the living room to the sliding glass door. The cold wind whipped in around me and I tried to close it quickly so my sister didn't get cold. My mom was already reaching into the crib wrapping a blanket around her. My brother was waving at me at the window. He went to plaster his face against the glass but it must have been too cold because he jerked away from it. Whiskey was meowing at the door I had just closed. I walked towards the mailbox where the bus would stop. I stood waiting in the cold.

The week I came back was the best week ever for Mrs. Eden's Super Supermarket. Each week her prizes had a theme. One week earlier that year the prizes were stuffed animals. The girls went crazy over them. I did, too. The boys pretended they didn't care but I caught Jason holding the stuffed lion every now and then. Another week earlier that year, the prizes had to do with school so there were special pencils and erasers. She even had a few of those plastic things the students could use to make sure they held their pencils correctly. I told Mrs. Eden I hated them and told her why. She just said that it could be like the anthem. I just do what is best for me as long as I'm doing my best work.

This week, all the things she had for sale were items we could use in a magic show. There was a top hat, a deck of cards, trick dice, a long magic wand, a stuffed white rabbit, rings that strung together but easily came apart, long handkerchiefs, and a flower that squirted water. The class went crazy trying to behave as best as they could to earn those table points. Each prize cost a certain amount of the marbles we earned at our table.

It was a Friday when I returned. We were winning. Jason's table had barely a handful of marbles. Tabitha told me that Jason was getting into a lot of trouble while I was gone. Vicky was still begging to switch from Jason's table when I returned. Eric's table wasn't doing any better, but my table was almost overflowing. Vicky was the Cup Keeper for her table and when it was time to count, she didn't even bother. Eric's table still added up their marbles, and were trying to act

213

like angels the whole day, but it didn't work. Kyle, our Cup Keeper, proudly announced our total: thirty-seven.

It was a new record for the year. Mrs. Eden called Kyle first, as she was the Cup Keeper. She got to go up and use some of the marbles to buy the items. Next week, Mrs. Eden was going to fill the empty spots with new items for next week's table. The competition to be the best behaved was getting fierce. Kyle went up next, and came back with the Top Hat. It had a purple and blue haze to it. She tilted it on her head. Only a little bit of her short, blonde hair stuck out.

"Who did you pick to be next week's Cup Keeper?" Mrs. Eden asked.

Kyle pointed to Scott.

"Okay," Mrs. Eden said, showing off her wares, "Scott, it's your turn."

Scott went up and came back with the squirting flower. I secretly wanted that, but felt glad he got it instead of some of the other boys.

"Scott," Mrs. Eden called, "pick the next person at your table to come up, please."

"Tabitha," Scott said and looked at me. "It's only because you haven't been here all week. I think she should choose next."

I smiled and nodded and watched Tabitha go up the Super Supermarket. I turned to my table and said, "I bet you she's going to pick the rabbit."

Tabitha turned back towards us snuggling the stuffed white rabbit. Kyle, Scott and I laughed as I called out, "I totally knew you were going to get that."

Tabitha shrugged, "What? It's cute!"

I agreed and sighed. I secretly wanted the stuffed white rabbit too.

Mrs. Eden called, "Mike, you're up!"

"Hey!" Eric whined, "that's not fair. He hasn't even been here."

"Yeah," Jason added, "he shouldn't get a turn!"

Mrs. Eden gave them both a look and they sunk down into their seats. Vicky slammed her head down into the table dramatically.

I went up and looked at what was left over, and grinned. I knew exactly what I wanted. I picked up the magic wand.

"The magic wand?" Mrs. Eden winked. "Good choice."

"I secretly wanted this the whole time," I said, and hugged it as I went back to the table.

At the end of the day, Mrs. Eden had us pack up and gathered us to the rainbow carpet. "This year is almost ending with only a few more months to go and it's important to remember that we all need to work together. We've had a wonderful year. One of the best, in my opinion, but it won't stay that way if we don't remember to treat each other with respect. We don't have to like each other, but we do have to respect each other. Respecting someone is harder to do, but has the most rewards."

She asked us to stand and line up at the door. "One more thing ..."

We all stopped and looked at her. She grinned, "Next week I'm changing the tables around just a little bit."

"Thank goodness!" Vicky exclaimed, throwing her hands up in the air, as we all headed out to the buses, or to walk home or to getting picked up by our families. I couldn't wait to show my brother my new magic wand.

I wasn't allowed to play with the wand indoors. For the rest of the winter, I had to watch that magic wand just sit in the corner of our room collecting dust not magic. When the snow finally thawed away and the weather became drier, Christopher and I walked out of the house. The wand was almost as long as my legs, so it felt more like a magic staff. It was completely black accept for the two white tips on both ends of the stick.

I held out my right hand and pointed the magic wand at it as I copied what The Amazing Mumford said on Sesame Street, "Abracadbra! A la peanut butter and jelly sandwich!"

No peanut butter and jelly sandwich appeared. The magic spell hardly worked on Sesame Street either.

"Christopher," I said, in an exciting and mysterious voice, holding the wand up above me with both hands like I was He-Man, "This is The Magic Wand of Invisibility. I am going to make you … DISAPPEAR!"

He squealed and ran away. I chased after him and we ran around the yard pretending to be magicians. I was a great magician who was teaching his apprentice new tricks, but both of us were trying to find the most powerful spell in the universe.

"Apprentice Christopher," I said in a big deep voice, "if we find the strongest spell in the universe, we will be unstoppable, and we will finally destroy the Shadow Monster!"

"When can I play with it?" he asked, eagerly eyeing the wand.

"When I can make you," I began, waving my arms and the wand around wildly, "DISAPPEAR!"

"Where is the strongest spell?" he asked, holding his hands up.

"The strongest spell in all the universe? The most powerful sorceress in the world has it," I explained. "She is an ancient creature who only gives the spell to greatest magicians."

"Who is she?"

"Her name," I began, getting more excited, "is the Sorceress WHISKEY!"

"Your cat?" he gasped. "I never knew that about her."

I laughed and continued to wave the wand wildly. "She only comes when we say her magic words."

"Kitty?" he asked.

I nodded, "Well done, my apprentice. Yes. Four times we must call to her. Are you ready?

My brother nodded eagerly, and I turned to the woods and waved my magic wand. "Here, kitty, kitty, kitty, kitty!"

My brother waved his hands towards the woods too, and we both called out, "Kitty, kitty, kitty, kitty!"

A small meow came from behind us and, as we turned, Whiskey was sitting on the back steps looking at us like we had lost our marbles.

"I get it!" I exclaimed. "Losing our marbles!"

I laughed as Whiskey turned away from us and began rolling around on the top step. She rolled around too much and fell down the rest. I laughed and she sat like a queen and licked her paw like nothing happened.

"Tell us the magic!" my brother yelled, darting at her. She looked at him quickly and gave a startled meow with a purr mixed in.

"WAIT!" I shouted, and my brother stopped. He turned back to me. "That's it! She told us the spell." I copied her meow with a purr mixed in. "Prreowr."

"That's it?" Christopher said.

"Now I can make you disappear!"

My brother squealed and ran up to me. I told him to stand still as I said the spell.

I started, "Abracadabra. A LA KAZAM!"

I spun the wand up in the air with a powerful look in my face. My brother grinned and clapped his hands. His eyes were round with excitement.

The wand spun in my left hand and I held it tightly as I lowered quickly, ending the spell, "PRREOWR!"

I felt a thud and I immediately let go of the wand. Christopher fell hard on his backside and immediately began to scream horrifically. His little hands shot up to his right eye and blood poured out between his fingers. I froze. I couldn't move. I didn't know what to do. His screams shocked me. I heard the back door slam open and my mom running down the steps.

"What is going on here?!" she yelled. Christina was still in her arms. She, too, was crying. I looked at my little sister and wondered if my spell had hurt her too. I began to tremble. My stomach felt so sick. I raised my fingers to my mouth and just stood there staring at all the blood pouring down my little brother's face.

And that's when I heard the roar. It came from the house. I heard something pound down the stairs. I heard it tremble through the living room. I heard it go through the kitchen. The back door whipped open again, and he stood at the top of the stairs in his comfy shorts and roared.

"I AM TRYING TO SLEEP!" he howled. "What is going on?"

My mom was screaming as well, trying to both hold Christina and examine Christopher's face.

She took a breath exasperated, "Mike, what did you do?!"

My dad was like a train travelling across the yard. I could feel his footsteps in the ground beneath me. I cowered back, and he saw Christopher and then came for me. His hand dug into my arm and he wrangled me around, screaming the same question over and over again. Telling me to answer him.

"What did you do, Mike? What did you do? Answer me!"

I wailed at first until I realised he wasn't going to stop until I answered him. I opened my mouth and all I could say was, "I tried to make him disappear."

"A centimetre lower and he would have lost his eye," the doctor said at the hospital later, putting the last of the little white strips on my brother's eyebrow. "Son, I think your magic days are over."

He chuckled a bit and so did our mom. Christopher was still trying to chatter away about what had happened. "And then Whiskey told us the magic spell and Mike tried it. But it was bad. It was very bad."

My dad was silent most of the time except to ask questions about the eye. He'd try to laugh but I could see in his eyes he wasn't happy.

On our way home, my mom looked back at me and said, "You are very lucky he wasn't seriously hurt."

My brother had a sucker in his mouth. It was round and red and one of my favourite candies, but I knew I didn't deserve one.

I looked at my brother and placed my forehead against the side of his arm. I rubbed it like Whiskey rubbed her head against me. "I'm so sorry, Christopher."

I looked up at him to see if he was mad. He pulled out his sucker and pointed it at me. He grinned, but all I could see were the small white strips that covered his gash.

I turned away and heard him pop the candy back into his mouth. The rest of the ride was silent accept for Christopher enjoying his sucker and dad puffing on his cigarette. He'd already said he wasn't going into work.

"I'll miss another shift because my eldest son, my firstborn, can't behave," he grumbled.

I remembered when dad called me a curse and I looked down at my feet and wondered, yet again, if he was right.

I didn't want the school year to end. I tried to find out from Mrs. Eden who my teacher was going to be next year, but she shrugged, "They're changing the teachers around a bit, Mike. I really don't know. Trust me, I would tell you. I know you're worried."

I nodded. I hadn't told anyone about what I did to my brother. I didn't tell anyone that my dad had a bonfire and used gasoline to make sure the magic wand burnt into ash.

"Why can't you be my teacher forever?" I asked Mrs. Eden.

She thought about her answer for a while and picked up a pencil from her desk. "You see this pencil?"

I nodded.

"A pencil is just a pencil. Eventually, each usage will take it away. You'll have to find another pencil. And eventually, that pencil will go away too. Nothing lasts forever, Mike. You know this more than anyone."

"I just won't use the pencil," I said, crossing my arms.

Mrs. Eden smiled, "What's the point of having a pencil if you aren't going to use it? How would you write your stories?"

Mrs. Eden was right, but I didn't want her to be.

She handed her pencil over to me. "Write. No matter what kind of different pencils you get, use them to write your stories. You write fantastic stories. Promise me you'll write your stories."

I promised.

Mrs. Eden looked at the time and rang her handbell from her desk. Everyone stopped what they were doing. Our desks had been put into rows the last few weeks of school. We didn't have tables anymore. Each of our desks had its own cup with our names on it. We each had to earn our own marbles. We were to take the cups home with us on the last day of school.

And there we were, the last time she was going to tell us to pack our bags. She called each one of us by name and told us to bring our cups, grab our bags and line up at the door. With each one of us, she put in a brand new bag of marbles into our cups.

"Make sure not to lose your marbles," she chuckled a bit and used her handkerchief to dab away the tears in her eyes.

I laughed, "Don't worry, Mrs. Eden, we won't lose our minds."

She winked at me.

When the last bell of the day rang, she shooed us out the door. I was last. I made sure of it. I allowed others to cut in front of me. I stopped at the door and looked up at her. She smiled down at me.

"What if my teacher next year is mean?" I asked.

"Then you'll do what Mike does best," she smiled. "You'll survive. And you'll write your stories about it. I'm sure of it."

I smiled and gave her one last hug.

Mrs. Eden held me, and when I looked up at her, she ran her hand up along my face and moved the bangs from my eyes. "Your grandmother would be so proud of you."

That night, my father took me aside. I could smell his drink on his breath mixed in with the ashes that flicked at me from his cigarette. My mom wasn't home. Christina and Christopher were already in bed.

He coughed in my face and hissed as he grabbed my arm, "Tonight. When I cough three times, you will come out of your room and peek out into the living room. I want you to see something."

I shuttered as he let me go. "Three coughs. If I don't see you, you'll be in trouble."

His face grew closer to me until I could feel the ash flick into my face and feel the warmth of his stench. He pushed me towards my bedroom and closed the door until only a small gap was showing.

"Don't fall asleep. Listen."

I crawled into bed. Whiskey was already on the bed stepping off the covers until I crawled underneath them. She nuzzled my neck and wrapped her front legs around it. I hugged her back. I could still smell him on me. I could still feel his cigarette against my face. I flicked on a flashlight I had beneath my pillow and pulled out one of my favourite comics, Uncanny X-Men #101, and flipped through the pages. The X-men were my favourite comics now. They were a bunch of people with extraordinary gifts who didn't fit in with the rest of the world. I was just like them. I turned to my favourite page. Jean Gray was now The Phoenix.

"Out of the ashes," I whispered to Whiskey, "We will rise."

THE END OF BOOK ONE

I recognised the lady from the last church we went to. She had shaded glassed she wore on a chain much like my Grandma Boyer did sometimes. She wore a dark flowered dress and made baby noises to my sister in the cart.

Christina was watching me though and had rolled her head away and looked up at the lady with wide eyes. I imagined my sister thinking, "Woah, who are you and why are you touching my cheeks?"

Everyone touched her cheeks. They were rosy and chubby. I liked kissing each one and watching her eyes light up and grin up at me. If I wasn't careful though, she'd swing her hands in excitement and punch me in the face.

My brother had chubby cheeks but I didn't kiss them. He'd always scrunch his nose up and wipe the kisses away saying, "Ew, gross."

"That is a cute little bow," the lady grinned, pointing to a little bow pinned into the thick head of hair my sister was already growing.

My mom said she was probably going to have hair like mine, brown and thick. She hoped my sister didn't get the unruly wavy hair my mother had or the short curly hair my brother had. My brother couldn't have long hair. Instead of growing straight it was curl up quickly.

When my dad came back with other things he needed to have at home, he joined in the pleasant chat with the lady from church. My brother was holding hands with my mom trying to get away. My sister kept following me with her eyes so I'd try to hide behind adults or stands that held food products the store was trying to sell.

I noticed my dad's charming smile. It used to make me smile, too. It used to make me feel safe, but now it just made me feel sick. He'd flash his teeth and give a deep comforting laugh at whatever the adults were talking about. He had two teeth on either side of the top row that were longer than the rest. I sometimes pretended he was a vampire. He did hate the mornings and was much more comfortable in the night.

The adults didn't come up to me at school though. No one really did, but that was probably because my parents weren't with me. I rode the yellow bus to school alone and did the same as I walked up the sidewalk into the school. I would see the cars in the drop off zone pull up and sometimes a parent would get out and walk their child to the doors. Other times they'd hug or kiss at the door. I always imagined them to be so happy.

"Have a good day, John," the father would say with bright eyes and an excited voice, "And remember, I love you."

"Oh gee, I love you too, dad," the son would say and give his father a huge hug before skipping into school. HIs school bag would be full of lollies and lunches. He'd have a ton of toys.

The mother would jump out of the car and chase after her son, "Johnny, wait!"

The son would stop and turn around, "Yes, mother?"

"I just missed you already and decided I wanted to walk you to the door."

"Oh mother, I already miss you too! Let's go to school together!" the son would say and they'd hold hands and skip their way to the door.

Someone bumped into the side of me as I had stopped in the middle of the sidewalk and watched this imaginary family go into the school. I blinked my eyes and shook my head.

I looked back my yellow bus with our bus driver, Tammy. She was chewing her bubble gum into bubbles and popping them loudly as she snapped, "Hurry up and get off the bus! If you're late, it's on you not me!"

She peered out at me through her large glasses and popped another bubble. I decided to wave at her wildly and with a big smile say, "Have a good day, Tammy!"

Tammy titled her head and then watched the last kid come off the bus before she pulled the door closed and drove off shaking her head.

"Okay, bye, Tammy, I already miss you!" I shouted. I mean, I didn't really. We never spoke unless she was yelling at me to sit down in my seat before she pulled away from my driveway.

It was usually the bigger kids who were last off the bus. They weren't in a hurry to get to school and most of them seemed to be unhappy all the time. Maybe 4th and 5th grade was awful? I was hoping school would get better as I got older, but it didn't seem like it.

Somehow, I ended up being the last one to walk up the sidewalk after everyone else even though I was usually the first one off the bus. The yellow bus was not fun, unless Tammy was in the mood for her country music and had it on full blast as her own curly black hair bobbed and danced down the dirt roads. She'd being going a bit faster to the music and a lot of us sitting near the seats closest to the wheels would be bouncing up and down.

I started walking again and put on my best smile. I was told I had a nice smile, too. Sometimes I was told it was like my father's and that would scare me, but I wanted to smile. Smiles were safe.

Third grade. I already knew the name of my teacher because we got a letter in the mail. I had a Ms. West and my room number was 3W. I wished they included a map because I hated walking into the school and trying to guess where the classroom was, but maybe it was a game for the teachers?

I had to ask my mom, "What is a Ms.?"

My mom finished reading the letter we got from the school and ruffled my hair, "What?"

"Missus is a girl and mister is a boy. So, what is a Mizz? Does it mean both?"

My mom's eyes widened and she left her hand on top of my head, "Oh my gosh, Mike, no. Missus is when a girl is married. Mizz is when she was married but not anymore."

"Why?"

My mom let go of my head and folded up the letter and placed it on the dining room table where my parents put all paper stuff. We couldn't even eat at the table anymore, but that was okay because we had tv trays that we folded open and sat in front of us and ate off of when watching tv.

"Her husband probably passed away."

"Like Grandma Boyer?" I asked, hugging my mom from the side.

"Yes."

"Oh, poor Ms. West."

"Remember Miss Young?" she asked me.

I nodded and curled my lip up, "Do I have to?"

My mom laughed, "She's called a Miss because she hasn't married yet."

"Oh, so Mister means a guy is married. So what's he called when he's not?"

My mom thought a bit, "Mister."

"What's it called when his wife passes away?"

She thought a bit longer, "A widower. And a woman is a widow."

"I thought she was a Mizz."

"They're both correct."

"So, I'm a Mister?"

"No, you're a boy."

"I'm so confused."

About The Author

Michael Stoneburner grew up in the United States but now lives in Australia. As a child, he always wanted to be a writer but was told to get a real job, so he was a primary teacher for nearly 10 years. Michael, however, is defiant and currently focusing his attention on his writing while drinking coffee. When he's not writing, he's hanging out at the comic store, enjoying a good cafe or exploring the natural world around him. You can also find his thoughts on Twitter @evilgeniustobe or see what he's up to on Instagram @eyesofstone or even go on Facebook @themichaelstoneburner and see what else he's promoting!